Outrageous Prayer
David Freitag

Published by David Freitag
Newberg, Oregon

Outrageous Prayer
Copyright © 2013
David Freitag

ISBN 978-1-61422-984-1

Printed in the US by Instantpublisher.com

Acknowledgments

This book is the result of several years work and would not have been either written or published without the help of numerous people. I want to thank my daughter, Sara, for her countless hours helping me edit the manuscript. My wife, Donelle, has been a constant encouragement to me to pursue writing. My friend, Pastor Galen Gingerich, gave me great encouragement after reading an early draft of the manuscript and asking me to teach it at our church New Horizons in McMinnville, Oregon.

I pray that this book will encourage those who read it to pursue a closer relationship with Jesus and our Heavenly Father.

Table of Contents

Foreword

Imagine gaining fresh insight about prayer that will empower you to radically represent Jesus Christ to everyone in your sphere of influence. Jesus modeled a lifestyle of intimate relationship with the Father where He found peace, refreshment and strength in His presence, and would then step into the flow of people's lives, forgiving their sin and releasing the power of heaven in signs, wonders, and miracles. Jesus and His disciples shifted the spiritual atmosphere of their region of the world through the declaration and the re-introduction of God's Kingdom.

Outrageous Prayer is enlightening, inspiring, and calls the heart of God-lovers into fresh, passionate encounters with Him and reveals the relationship of sons and daughters who no longer approach prayer with passivity, but with bold and confident declaration. This book is thought provoking and may challenge traditional paradigms regarding the teachings of Jesus concerning prayer throughout the Gospels.

The spiritual revelation shared in this book came to the mind and heart of my dear friend, David Freitag, one who is not willing to settle for the status quo of past experience, but one who is continually in pursuit of intimately knowing and more fully representing Jesus and the advancement of His Kingdom on the earth.

In my personal library, I have over fifty books on the subject of prayer, including the classics, all which have enriched my life. David's teachings on *Outrageous Prayer* have enlarged my understanding, energized, and augmented my personal life and have impacted the lives of many of our congregation. This book will be included in our School of Ministry and used in training of our prayer teams. I highly recommend this book to every believer who wants to expand their spiritual foundation and who are willing to explore the possibilities of relationship with our Father in prayer and representing Him to our world. Enjoy!

Galen Gingerich
Senior Leader, New Horizons Church

Introduction

Over my years as a pastor, it was not uncommon to hear people asking how to pray. Their question resembled the command/request that one of the twelve disciples posed to Jesus in Luke 11:1. "Teach us to pray like John taught his disciples." Jesus responded with what we now call the Lord's Prayer. This prayer is curiously simple compared with the disciples' longing for knowledge. Frankly, for many years I considered Jesus' response a bit disappointing. If I were one of the disciples listening to Jesus I would desire a "deeper" lesson on prayer. Shouldn't Jesus' response to such a deep question have been more profound? Yet, what made the Lord's Prayer so special in the disciples' eyes? Perhaps I've taken this simple prayer for granted and missed something important. When I began to study further the Lord's Prayer, I discovered that it is quite outrageous. In a sense, Jesus' teaching on prayer exploded my "black box" of traditional prayer.

In his prayer instruction, Jesus began with what might have been strange to the disciples. As Jews, they would have been familiar with praying to God as "Lord," but Jesus commanded them to address God as "Our Father." Today this does not sound strange because prayers are frequently addressed to God as Father, but to the Jews this was unthinkable. In fact, there is not one instance in the Old Testament of a prayer addressed to God as Father. Fatherhood is implied in 2 Chronicles 7:14, when God revealed that His people would be called by "His name." We can only be called by God's name if He is our Father or Husband, because these are the two means by which a name is passed on. God told David that He would be a Father to Solomon, David's son. On other occasions, God revealed himself as a Father and Creator of humanity. God called the Messiah His son in Psalm 2:7.

When Jesus referred to God as Father, although he could point to Psalm 2:7, the Jews still plotted to kill him because his address raised him to an equal status with God. Not only did

Introduction

Jesus refer to God as his own Father, but he also commanded the disciples to pray to God as their Father. If Jesus' own referral to God as Father was unacceptable to the Jews, how much more would it offend them for the disciples to address God in the same manner? What point is Jesus making by using the title "Father" in prayer?

Upon examination of the Lord's Prayer in both Matthew 6 and Luke 11, another question arises. Why did Jesus teach his disciples to pray by primarily using commands rather than requests? Since the New Testament was originally written in Greek, what might be learned from the Greek use of commands? For example how do we account for the Greek imperative (command) being used? Greek scholars have noted the unusual usage of the imperative in the New Testament. The ancient Greeks regarded the imperative form as inappropriate to use with superiors.[1] Modern grammars of New Testament Greek interpret imperatives used in prayer as a form of request or asking permission, but this explanation does not address the reluctance in ancient Greek to use the imperative in addressing a superior. The question arises: if the imperative merely reflected asking permission and not necessarily a command, then why was it not used in communication with a superior in Greek culture? Furthermore, on what basis do we interpret a command as asking permission and when is it truly a command? For example, if it is possible to interpret imperatives as asking permission, then how do we know Jesus is not merely giving us permission to love one another as he has loved us (John 13:34), rather than issuing us a command to do so? To a Greek-speaking first century reader of the New Testament, the abundant use of the imperative in the disciples' speech to Jesus and in prayer to God, must have been shocking. At the very least, the New Testament writers were pushing boundaries by using Greek imperatives to describe their relationship with Jesus and with Father. Furthermore, the disciples' request/command of Jesus raises a question. Why would they ask Jesus to teach them to pray? They were Jews

Introduction

who would have been familiar with the Psalms and the prayers found in them. John the Baptist had taught his disciples to pray; some of them may have previously been disciples of John, or were at least familiar with his teaching. Yet with their background in prayer, they still made this request to Jesus. We have to wonder what made Jesus' prayer so different and attractive to his disciples? They desired to pray in a manner similar to Jesus, apparently different from what they had ever encountered. If that is true, then we should be looking at the Lord's Prayer and seeking to answer what makes this prayer unique from the model of prayer found in the Psalms and from what John taught his disciples.

Surprisingly, Jesus' disciples themselves issued a command that he teach them to pray. In response, Jesus gave them a model prayer in which they were to issue a series of commands to Father. Jesus could have given this prayer in another form, such as a list of requests. The Lord's prayer is a surprising prayer considering that God is the highest superior anyone can engage. Jesus instructed his disciples to address Him in a manner in which the Greeks would never address a superior. Today we categorize these prayers as requests, but this is not how first century readers would have seen them. They may have made requests using commands to peers or subordinates, God is neither. They would not have used an imperative to address a superior, making the prayer of the Christian very different than the prayer of a Jew or that of a Roman or Greek. What are the resulting implications for us as Christians? What is God seeking to teach us about prayer in relation to His Kingdom? How does this instruction change our view of God's nature and our relationship with Him?

Chapter 1
Jesus' command to pray

A father driving his family home, asks his teenage daughter if she knows how to get home. Knowing that she will soon be learning to drive, he wants to know if she is aware of her surroundings. He instructs her to tell him when to turn. She begins by saying, "turn right here?" Her father responds with "are you telling me or asking me?" She changes the tone of her voice and declares, "Turn right here!" Then she proceeds to successfully issue him a series of commands which leads them directly home. Pleased, the father knows that his daughter has passed this "little quiz." Rather than being displeased, the father is content that his daughter succeeded, even if her commands might seem inappropriate without the proper context. The fact that a teenage girl felt comfortable issuing her father commands reveals something about her relationship with him. Further, the father's instruction that she issue him commands reveals something about his view of their relationship. Only in a context of trust and intimacy could this take place.

A Command

As a parallel, the example Jesus set by issuing commands to the Father reveals something about our relationship with him and with Father in heaven, in that it is of a familial and intimate nature. Because his teaching came before the cross and he opened the way to the Father, Jesus' prayer instruction foreshadowed a level of intimacy he would like his followers to experience with the Father.

In Matthew 6:9, Jesus' instruction to pray was not a recommendation or suggestion, but a command. Since they were his followers, they were to imitate him in his teaching and lifestyle. The Christian faith was more than a curriculum with a reading list and projects to accomplish. It was more than a philosophy to follow. Jesus taught his disciples to follow

5

(imitate) the way that he lived. That included the way that Jesus prayed. As is implied with the word, "prayer," Old Testament prayer was directed to God. However, the Jews prayed to God as a member of the covenant people, not as individuals. Since Abraham, the friend of God, was their father, they had access to God in prayer. Abraham had a right relationship with Him through being considered righteous on account of his faith. The devout Jew could pray with a firm confidence in God, because he could count Abraham as his father. Therefore, he knew that God heard his prayers. But even so, the Jew was relationally removed from God. He always needed a mediator, the priest.

In contrast to the Jews, worshipers of other gods had a different approach to prayer. The prophets of Baal tried to convince Baal to respond by cutting themselves, because they were not sure whether he heard them or was in the mood to respond. They pleaded and used self-abasement as a means to convince or even manipulate a god who might be unwilling to assist them. They had to make a convincing case to catch Baal's attention. In contrast, Elijah did no such thing. He made a simple request and saw God respond, because God was faithful to His promises sealed by the covenant He made with His people. True and false prayer are distinguished by either coming from the heart or being lip-service. When prayer slipped into a religious exercise or a religious task to be accomplished, God rejected the prayers of His people, because their heart was not with Him (Isaiah 29:13-14).

The New Testament model of prayer follows the Old Testament model. However, contrary to Old Testament times, the Christian does not pray as merely a member of a covenant people, but he comes based on his personal faith and commitment to Jesus. The Christian enters into prayer as though he were Jesus himself, because Scripture declares that he is "in Christ" and even seated in the heavenly places (Ephesians 2:6). Through Jesus, access to God in prayer was opened to all peoples, not just a particular people (Acts 10:45). Since a person can enter into a personal relationship with Jesus, prayer is a dialogue rather than a monologue. The believer waits silently to hear from the Lord, a practice even taught in the Old Testament (Ecclesiastes 5:1). Through prayer, the Holy Spirit may also give specific direction (Acts 13:2-3). Furthermore, prayer implies a faith relationship in which the believer expects God to hear and respond to his prayers.

A believer asks God for wisdom to guide his actions in a particular situation (James 1:5). Some time later, ideas may pop into his head which had never occurred to him; but address the situation in question. He may assume that they were the fruit of his own creative ability. However, the astute follower of Jesus recognizes that these are not ideas he could have invented. How does he account for them? The ideas are sent from his heavenly Father, through the Holy Spirit.

Why pray?

Through the Gospel of Luke we understand the background that led to Jesus giving the Lord's prayer (Luke 11:1-2). One of the disciples came to Jesus and issued a command, "teach us to pray." One thing that we learn from Jesus' model prayer is that he commanded them to pray in a bold manner. Such a prayer indicates the intimacy a believer has with Father, because one does not typically speak in such a direct manner unless there exists a very close relationship.

Because of Jesus' teaching on prayer, the believer does not come to God the Father as a beggar hoping to convince him to do what is right or good. Rather, he comes as a beloved child, whom God the Father loves and delights in doing what is needed. Jesus is not in any way describing a formal relationship, but one that is familial and close. When we understand that

Jesus' Command To Pray

Jesus has given his followers the command and authority to make disciples, then they also have the right to direct the Father to provide for their needs in order to fulfill his commission and proclaim the Gospel to all nations (Matthew 24:14; 28:18-20).

Not only do we pray because Jesus commanded and taught us to pray, but through prayer we can be a blessing to others. Through our prayers, we assist others in their tasks. Paul requested that the Thessalonians pray with him for the purpose of spreading the Gospel through Silas, Timothy and himself. Paul also had them pray so that Silas, Timothy and he would be rescued from evil men, specifically those men who do not have faith (2 Thessalonians 3:1-2). The Thessalonians were in one location, but their influence through prayer extended through the actions of Paul and his co-laborers.

While prayer can impact the results of an individual's actions, it can also impact the individual himself, both physically and spiritually. In James 1:2-7, James urged his readers, who were enduring difficulty, to pray. Prayer should be the natural response of any and every believer who encounters difficulty in life. If that difficulty is sickness, then he is to seek out the elders so that they will pray for and anoint him with oil. Their faithful prayer restores the individual who is sick, weary or faint (James 5:15). James expanded his instruction from specifically elders to all believers. He went on to include confessing their sins and praying for one another in the process of healing. The word James used in verse sixteen is the typical word found in the New Testament for individuals receiving physical healing (James 5:13-16).

In order to encourage his readers, James implied that the great and powerful prophet Elijah was just like them. Elijah's prayer impacted nature for three and one half years. First through his prayer there was no rain, then after three and one half years, it poured down rain (James 5:17-18). Some have

Jesus' Command To Pray

assumed that prayers that produce physical healing or impacted nature were limited to another time, but James does not give us that option. He compared his readers, ordinary believers dispersed throughout the Roman Empire, to the great prophet Elijah. As James indicated, prayer can be a means of physical healing. Prayer also is the means by which people are freed spiritually. The disciples could not drive out the demon from the boy with seizures, even though Jesus had given the disciples the authority to cast out demons and heal the sick (Mark 6:7). Their inability to drive out the demon confused the disciples so they asked Jesus what the problem was. Jesus explained to them that certain types of demons could only come out with prayer. So in this case, although the disciples had authority over the demon, they still needed prayer to prepare them for the encounter. Curiously, when Jesus commanded the demon to leave, he did not take time to pray; he simply commanded the demon to leave. This account indicates that Jesus practiced a lifestyle of prayer. His teaching on this occasion indicated that His disciples were to practice the same type of prayer-lifestyle and understand their own authority in the spiritual world (Matthew 17:18; Mark 9:25, 29).

Prayer was the means of spiritual liberation for others. It was also a means to overcome temptation in the individual's life. As Jesus prayed in the Garden of Gethsemane, he urged his sleepy disciples to do the same, so that they would not fall into temptation (Luke 22:45). Earlier, Jesus had warned Peter about the battle he was about to encounter, but he failed to heed Jesus' warning (Luke 22:31-32). Later that evening, Peter would sadly deny that he even knew Jesus.

Meanwhile, Jesus went on through the power of prayer to withstand his trials before the Council and Pilate, as well as his ordeal on the cross. As Jesus faced his trials, he also forgave those who caused his suffering. Jesus' words to the disciples imply that prayer can indeed be a means for us to overcome

9

temptation. Specifically, Jesus' command to Peter indicates that if Peter had prayed and not slept, he could have overcome the temptation to deny Jesus.

Besides physical and spiritual liberation, prayer further defines the Christian and the Church. When describing the temple, Jesus declared it to be a house of prayer (Matthew 21:13). The temple was and is to be a place in which we meet and converse with God. Prior to the coming of the Spirit, the temple was a building, but after His coming, the temple became a people indwelt with the Spirit of God (1 Corinthians 3:16: 6:20). Since we are the people of God, we are to reflect that identity by prayer and communion with God.

Not only is prayer emphasized in the Gospels, but we continually observe the early church practicing corporate prayer, emphasized along with the apostles' teaching, fellowship and breaking of bread (the Lord's Supper/Communion) (Acts 2:42). The early church continued the Jewish custom of the hour of prayer at three PM (ninth hour) (Acts 3:1). The apostles viewed prayer as a fundamental part of their ministry along with the teaching of the word, so important that they delegated other important activities (Acts 6:4), so that they would not be distracted from prayer and the ministry of the word. For example, the apostles' decision to delegate the important role of food distribution revealed the high value they placed on prayer.

In times of crisis, the church gathered to prayer. During Peter's stay in prison, awaiting probable execution, the church gathered in a believer's home to intercede for him. This situation reveals the grace of God regarding prayer, even when there is lack of belief. Ironically, when God miraculously answered their prayer, they failed to believe it (Acts 12:5, 12-15). Prayer carries such great value, that the New Testament urges the believer to develop a life-style of continual prayer (Romans 1:9; 12:12; 15:30; 1 Corinthians 7:5; Ephesians 1:16; 6:18; Philippians 4:6;

Jesus' Command To Pray

Colossians 4:2; 1 Thessalonians 1:2; 5:17; 1 Timothy 5:5; Revelation 5:8; 8:3, 4). The New Testament reveals that prayer is one of the most important activities to which the Christian can give his time. Such a biblical emphasis on prayer reminds us that it is not a waste of our time, even though on certain occasions it may feel as if there are more important matters to which we could give our time.

Who/what we pray for

The breadth of our prayers is also surprising. Every believer is commanded to pray for his enemies, specifically those who persecute him (Matthew 5:44; Luke 6:27-28). Jesus' command is constructed in such a way that we are not merely to pray for our enemies once and call it good, but to continually pray for God's blessing upon their life. As Christians practice prayers of blessing upon those who hurt them, they reveal God's love to their enemies and experience His joy in their own life.

A blessing refers to praising or speaking well of someone. The believer is called to speak out the positive attributes of his enemy despite the pain of being mistreated. Part of blessing a person is praying that the individual would experience good from the hand of God. In this way, the believer demonstrates a lifestyle that reveals the very heart of God, but that is fundamentally different and contrary to the typical way of living.

As Jesus and Stephen prayed for God to forgive their tormentors, so also the believer is to do the same while enduring mistreatment. Since these are not suggestions from Jesus, but commands, the implication is that the blessings and prayers will be effective for the benefit of the enemy. This is not some backhanded way to to heap guilt upon the enemy, but is a genuine effort to bring good into their life despite the mistreatment suffered. The reason for such practice is not to end the mistreatment, but to experience what Jesus himself endured and what Paul referred to as the "fellowship of his suffering" (Philippians 3:10). As the believer prays for his enemies, Jesus reveals to him/her the same type of compassion that Jesus himself felt toward those who mistreated him. In this way, the believer draws closer to Jesus than he would have, had the difficulty never arisen.

In the New Testament, prayer was valued and sought after. Parents brought their young children to Jesus for prayer (Matthew 19:13). It is possible that they were seeking healing prayer for their children. In Mark 10:13 and Luke 18:15, we read that the parents brought them to be touched by Jesus. In the Gospels, this word, "touch" (haptomai), is found twenty-nine times. For the vast majority (twenty-five times), it is used for a touch that resulted in healing. The same word was used when the immoral woman touched Jesus at the Pharisee's house (Luke 7:39). However, this woman's encounter with Jesus resulted in her being healed spiritually (forgiven) (Luke 7:48). In any case, parents desired for Jesus to touch and pray for their children, indicating that they highly valued His prayer.

During Jesus' teaching in the Olivet Discourse, he indicated that prayer may change our future circumstances. He commanded his disciples to pray that, when it was necessary for them to flee from Jerusalem, it would not take place during winter or on a Sabbath (Matthew 24:20; Mark 13:18). The command being in the present tense indicates that the disciples were to pray continually for this future situation. If there were no chance of influencing a future event, then Jesus would not have commanded His disciples to pray in this manner.

Jesus could have made this a suggestion, but he didn't. He commanded his disciples to pray that their future take a certain course. This command indicates Jesus' concern for his disciples. He did not want them facing the difficulty of fleeing during the

Jesus' Command To Pray

winter or on a Sabbath. The command to pray reveals the loving concern that Jesus has for His followers. They would face the difficulty of fleeing, but he wanted that flight to be as manageable as possible. Jesus' command further implies that if they would pray for this, then the Father would grant their request.

When the Roman legions surrounded Jerusalem in 70 AD, the church historian, Eusebius, wrote that the Christians fled the city in obedience to what Jesus had told them.[2] Eusebius did not reveal the season, but that the flight was successful, indicating a favorable answer to their prayer.

In the Old Testament, Moses actually changed God's mind regarding a decision that God had determined to make. Moses interceded on behalf of Israel, even after God had commanded him to be quiet (Exodus 32:10-14). God commanded Moses to leave him alone so that He could destroy Israel for their sin of worshiping the golden calf. God wished to make Moses himself into a great nation. However, Moses ignored this command and intervened by calling God to remember his promise to Abraham, Isaac and Jacob, that he would multiply their descendants. Verse fourteen concludes that God changed his mind as a result of Moses' prayer.

In the Garden of Gethsemane, Jesus gave us other insights on the value of prayer. In Matthew 26:39, Jesus began his prayer with a conditional phrase, "if it is possible." The way the conditional is formed indicates that Jesus was not merely asking hypothetically, but that he assumed it was possible for the cup to be removed. Jesus' command "let this cup pass" (Mark formulates it as a request – Mark 14:35) indicates that it was Jesus' desire that the cup be removed from him. Therefore, the reason the cup was not removed was on account of the Father's purpose (Isaiah 53:10), not because it was impossible to be removed. Jesus' prayer in the Garden, as well as Moses' prayer found in Exodus 32, reveals that prayer is not a monologue during which we present a list of requests, but a dialogue in which we boldly reveal our heart and listen for God's response.

Jesus' final prayer in the garden gives us further insight into the prayer he commanded his disciples to pray in the Sermon on the Mount. Jesus commanded his disciples to pray that the Father's will be done on earth as it was in Heaven. In the Garden, Jesus expressed the desire/hope that the cup of suffering would pass from him (Matthew 26:39, 42), but in his next prayer, he submitted his desire to do the Father's will. Jesus prayed the exact prayer he had earlier commanded his disciples to pray, that the Father's will be done.

In Jesus' second prayer found in verse 42, Jesus submitted himself to the Father's will while laying his own will aside. Therefore, when we pray for the Father's will to be done on earth as it is in Heaven, we recognize that for the Father's will to be accomplished, we, like Jesus, may need to set aside our own will. On top of that, Jesus issued a command that the Father's will be done and in so doing, a corresponding command that not his own will be done. In this, Jesus models what it means to pray for the Father's will to be done on earth. We are to desire the Father's will, and even command it unconditionally, although it may mean that we will personally pay a high price for His will to be accomplished. Jesus lived out what it means to love the Lord God with all our heart, soul, mind and strength (Matthew 22:37). Jesus loved the Father and his will more than he loved his own life.

How to pray

Earlier in the Sermon on the Mount, Jesus gave instruction on how his followers should pray. When they prayed, they were to do so in a certain manner, not like the hypocrites, such as the

14

Jesus' Command To Pray

Pharisees (Matthew 6:5). The hypocrites prayed publicly because they desired to be seen and praised by men more than by God. They practiced the same false prayer found in the Old Testament, which was lip-service and not a heart response to God (Isaiah 29:13). Jesus taught the disciples not only how they were not to pray, but also how they were to pray (Matthew 6:6). In Matthew 23:14 and Mark 12:40, Jesus rebuked the Pharisees and Scribes for their man-focused prayer. Fundamentally, prayer was personal between the believer and God the Father. Therefore, Jesus instructed them to enter into a secret place, their inner room, to pray secretly with God. In this way, there was no possible way for men to praise them, because men had no idea what they were doing. The only one who could honor them was God the Father. By this practice, they would reveal that they desired to honor God more than receive honor from men. They were to pray to their heavenly Father, who sees what takes place in secret and will reward the praying believer.

Jesus' teaching on prayer reveals the fact that our relationship with God is personal. Spouses or close friends do not conduct their personal conversations with each other in public; rather they find a private place to speak with one another. In fact most people find it uncomfortable and inappropriate when spouses have their personal conversations in public. The Pharisees' public practice of prayer indicated that from their perspective, their relationship with God was not all that personal.

Some have concluded from Jesus' teaching on prayer, that he was condemning all public prayer, but that was not his point. Jesus did not teach his disciples to avoid public prayer, but to avoid praying publicly in order to be seen by men. Jesus was always concerned with the heart's intentions. If Jesus had prohibited public prayer, he himself would have violated his own command when he prayed publicly on various occasions. Before calling the weary to follow him, Jesus publicly praised the Father for revealing truth to children and hiding it from the wise and

15

Jesus' Command To Pray

intelligent (Matthew 11:25-27). Outside the tomb of Lazarus, Jesus publicly thanked the Father for hearing him (John 11:41-42). He publicly asked the Father to forgive the soldiers who crucified him (Luke 23:34). He later prayed that the Father receive his soul. Jesus' example reveals that he did not condemn public prayer; rather, he condemned the desire to be honored by men rather than God, the Father.

A second model of prayer to avoid was that of the Gentiles, whose prayers followed what the prophets of Baal practiced in 1 Kings 18:2-29. The Baal prophets called on the name of Baal over and over from morning until noon, hoping that he would respond because of their repetition. The second half of the day, they cried louder and cut themselves, thinking that they could somehow capture Baal's attention. They believed that they needed to convince him of their devotion in order to get a response. Jesus taught that God does not need convincing; He is a loving Father who delights in listening to the prayers of His children. In fact, He knows our need before we ask, or even before we know of that need (Matthew 6:8).

However, Jesus did teach that his followers are to persevere in prayer. For this reason he told the parable of the persistent widow. His point was not that we need to convince God of our need, but that we must learn to persevere and pursue a prayer relationship with the Father. Jesus concluded his teaching by asking whether He would find faith on the earth when he comes. In other words, will Jesus find His people exercising their belief and faith in God through prayer when He returns (Luke 18:1-8)? The purpose of persistent prayer is not that our Father needs to be informed. It is that we need to be strengthened in our persistent asking and reminded of our dependent relationship, lest we conclude that we do not need our Father.

The third prayer error Jesus addressed reveals a mistaken view of God's nature. What loving Father would be pleased if

Jesus' Command To Pray

his children had to beg him and torture themselves thinking that this was the only way he would respond to their request? The begging of Baal's prophets revealed that they did not consider Baal to be loving or benevolent. On the other hand, Jesus taught that our Father in heaven responds to our needs because he loves us.

Matthew recorded that Jesus commanded his disciples to pray in a bold, authoritative manner. In Mark 11:24, Jesus added the command to exercise faith (belief) when praying. Jesus commanded the disciples to believe that they will receive. This is not a blank check type of prayer. Jesus made a request of the Father, that the cup would pass from Him, but He did not receive what He had prayed to the Father. Lack of belief was not a problem for Jesus, so that could not be the reason why Jesus' request was not granted. Although Jesus had faith, the Father's plan and purpose determined the final outcome.

We are to pray for the specifics mentioned in the Lord's prayer. Since Jesus commanded us to pray in those areas, it is safe to assume that the Lord's prayer reflects the Father's heart, and that these requests will be granted. Therefore, we are to believe that God's name is holy, for his kingdom to come, for his will is done on earth as it is in heaven. We believe that our daily bread is provided, that our sins are forgiven, that we are delivered from evil. Since Jesus already commanded us to pray boldly in these areas, then we should believe that we will receive them. In those areas that reflect our will, we should also take time to inquire of the Father's heart, so that we can pray in accordance with Him as Jesus did in the Garden.

As in the Lord's Prayer, Jesus taught his disciples the importance of forgiveness so that the Father would forgive them (Mark 11:24-25). In the Lord's Prayer, forgiveness of others was the measure for the Father to forgive the praying believers.

17

Jesus' Command To Pray

Paul urged the Thessalonians to pray without ceasing (1 Thessalonians 5:17). Paul's command indicates that prayer is to be a constant characteristic of the believer. This means that prayer is to be more like an ongoing conversation with God. The believer is to live with an awareness of God the Holy Spirit's presence with him, so that he can converse with him at all times. Because God is everywhere and we cannot escape his presence (Psalm 139:7), it is always possible to be in prayer with God. At no time is the believer alone, because the Spirit of God is always present with him and ready to provide him with help (Psalm 121:1).

 Instruction from Jesus and Peter imply that the conditions of our relationships with others impact our prayer relationship with our Heavenly Father. Peter taught his readers that a man's relationship with his wife can impact his prayers (1 Peter 3:7). Peter's instruction parallels Jesus' instruction about the necessity of forgiveness in regards to prayer. If we have broken relationships with others because of an unforgiving heart, or we fail to show honor to our wife, our communication with God the Father is hindered. Since we are all created in the image of God, He values each one of us; it is inconsistent for us to think we can maintain an open relationship with God, while at the same time justifying a broken relationship with someone else. God is a relational God; therefore to have an open relationship with Him requires that we do all that is in our power to have healthy relationships with others (Romans 12:18).

Results of prayer

Luke 3:21; 5:16; 6:12 give us a picture of how fundamental prayer was to Jesus' life. When Jesus was baptized, prayer was a part of that experience. As he prayed, heaven opened up to him. Luke 3:21 gives us a glimpse of how prayer can be a connection for us to heaven. Luke 5:16 and 6:12 indicate that prayer was a regular part of Jesus' life. On the other hand, Luke 6:12 describes a specific occurrence in Jesus' life, on that occasion . Jesus prayed throughout the night.

Out of the context of prayer, Jesus asked the most significant question of his ministry, "Who do the crowds say that I am?" (Luke 9:18) Jesus' question opened the door for Peter to confess him as Christ and reveal to Jesus that the Father had made Peter aware of Jesus' true identity (Luke 9:20). On the heels of Peter's confession, Jesus took three of his disciples on a prayer retreat (Luke 9:28-29). Like at Jesus' baptism, prayer provided the environment for a heavenly encounter. Jesus' prayer brought a heaven-like environment to the mountain-top, revealing Jesus glorified, along with Moses and Elijah. This account gives us a glimpse to what could happen as we make prayer a characteristic of our life.

In the Epistles, we find that prayer provides insight and knowledge useful for the church. In 1 Corinthians 14:13, Paul gave instruction to pray so that they would also know how to interpret messages given in tongues to the congregation. Paul's command reveals to us that we can pray in order to gain information and insight.

When Jesus commanded his disciples to pray in a certain manner (Matthew 6:9), he opened his disciples to a powerful and life-changing experience with God. Therefore, it is our mission to better understand the implication of each of the aspects of Jesus' model prayer.

Summary

Jesus' teaching on prayer in the Sermon on the Mount defined prayer for the rest of the New Testament and explained glimpses of intimate prayer found in the Old Testament. The foundation of prayer in the New Testament is an intimate relationship with God the Father. Our relationship is so close, familial and intimate with the Father that He even allows us to boldly issue Him commands. Jesus taught us to speak to the Father with a boldness and intimacy that the Greeks would never use with superiors. Since prayer is so intimate, it is to be primarily, although not exclusively, practiced in private. Since close friends and spouses do not avoid speaking in public, the child of God is not forbidden to speak with his Father in public; however his most intimate times with God will naturally be private in nature.

Prayer is also a conversation between two individuals, neither is obligated to do all that the other says. As a relational closeness is developed between the child and God the Father, more of what the individual prays will reflect the heart of God. However, God is also sovereign and not a puppet of our requests, so as our Father, He may decline legitimate requests of his children because he has something better or more timely in mind. From here, we will move on and examine the Lord's prayer in more detail one component at a time.

Questions for Reflection

1. Evaluate the times you pray. What motivates you to pray? While it is appropriate to pray out of need, how often do you pray simply because you desire to be with God?

2. To what extent might you have been impacted by the world's view of prayer? How often do you feel that you need to convince God to respond to your prayer?

3. When and where do you spend your secret times alone with your heavenly Father?

4. To what extent is prayer a continual aspect of your life?

Jesus' Command To Pray

How do you keep the Father's continual presence in the forefront of your mind?

Papa, I thank you for giving to me the privilege to address you personally because of what Jesus has done for me. Teach me to have an appropriate view of prayer and make it a continual aspect of my life. Amen.

Chapter 2
God Addressed As Father
Matthew 6:9

Years ago, I remember a child addressing his father with his father's first name as he heard others doing. I was quite impressed with the father's response. He reminded his son that of all the people on earth, only the son and siblings could refer to him as "dad," but anyone could call him by his name. Because of the closeness of their relationship, the child should not refer to his dad in a common manner, but hold on to his privileged position as son. I have always thought highly of that wise man's response. When we have the possibility of referring to someone as "Father," we are placed in a unique and privileged position. How we refer to someone reveals the closeness of our relationship with them. The more formal our response, the more distant the relationship and vice versa.

Growing up, we had close family friends. My sister and I were taught to refer to them as "uncle" and "aunt," even though we were not related to them. The familial titles revealed a closeness in the relationship between our two families. With other adults, we were always taught to use the title, "Mr" or "Mrs." In those cases, the more formal titles communicated to us that these individuals were not family or especially close personal friends.

During our years living in Rome, one of the constant questions was how we were to speak with people. In Italian, there is both a formal and informal manner of speech. When communicating with a new acquaintance or someone of higher social standing more formal language was used. However, a time would come, when the individual of higher social standing would communicate to the other person that they may use the informal with them. That shift indicated recognition of having reached a certain level of relational closeness. The decision to continue using formal language revealed the commitment to maintain relational distance, rather than accept the offered closer relationship. When we reflect upon it, the way we refer to another person communicates much of how we feel toward them.

God as Father

"Our Father in heaven ..." By referring to God as Father, Jesus immediately gave his disciples something to think about. In his own prayers, Jesus always referred to God as Father. The customary title for God among the Jews was "Lord." Not once is Jesus recorded using the title "Lord" to the Father in prayer. On the other hand, we have no examples of anyone in the Old Testament praying to God as Father. This distinction reveals how radical and controversial Jesus' teaching was to the religious Jews. Jesus' practice should not have been surprising to the disciples because, earlier in the Sermon on the Mount, he introduced them to the concept of God being their Father. Jesus told them that their good example would give glory to their Father in heaven (Matthew 5:15). By expressing love for their enemies, they would reveal themselves to be sons of their Father in heaven (Matthew 5:45). Practicing righteousness without regard to being honored by men would produce acknowledgment from their Father in heaven (Matthew 6:1, 4). Praying in solitude would cause their Father in heaven to recognize them (Matthew 6:6, 8). Refusal to forgive would remove their Father's forgiveness of them (Matthew 6:15; 11:25). Practicing fasting without being obvious about it brings heaven's reward (Matthew 6:18). Jesus reminded his disciples that, as they knew how to give good gifts to their children, so also their Father in heaven would give good gifts (Matthew 7:11).

Jesus went so far as to identify the Holy Spirit as the Spirit of their Father in heaven (Matthew 10:20). Jesus taught his disciples about their heavenly Father's detailed knowledge and care for them (Matthew 10:29).

24

God Addressed As Father

From the Jewish perspective, God was not Father; He was too remote and holy. They would not even pronounce His name for fear of being disrespectful. When Jesus identified God as his father, the Jews took offense because they believed it made him equal with God (John 5:17-18). Their response indicated that the concept of God as Father was foreign to the Jewish mind. The Jews tended to speak of God more formally, while identifying Abraham, Jacob or David as their father (forefather) (Luke 3:8; Mark 11:10; John 4:12).

Jesus did not correct the Jews' assessment of his equality with God. His lack of correction indicates that Jesus intended to communicate the implication that he was indeed equal to Father. Many use this lack of correction found in John 5:18 as a demonstration of the deity of Jesus. However, what is communicated when Jesus tells us that God is not only his Father, but his followers' Father as well? What is true of Jesus, is also true of his followers. If it was offensive for Jesus to call God his Father, how much more offensive would it be for Jesus to teach all his followers to address God as their Father?

An even more radical question remains. By Jesus teaching us to refer to Almighty God as Father, is he communicating that Father has lifted us up to his position along with himself? The simple reference to God as Father raises considerations about what Jesus has accomplished for us.

Jesus' instruction that the disciples address God as Father may shed light on what Paul declared about believers being seated in heavenly places (Ephesians 2:6). Peter declared that, through Christ, we have been made partakers of the divine nature (2 Peter 1:4). In this instance, the word Peter used for nature referred to the essential being of someone. God is divine by nature; man is human by nature. Yet, Peter declared that, through Jesus, a believer's nature is transformed from human to divine.

My Father

Throughout Jesus' ministry, he referred to God as his Father. Even at age twelve, Jesus understood that God was his Father. When rebuked by Mary for remaining in the temple, Jesus told her that he had to be in his Father's house (Luke 2:48-49). When clearing out the temple, again Jesus referred to it as his Father's house (John 2:16). Consistently in his prayers, Jesus referred to God as Father. Never did Jesus refer to God as "Lord," as would have been customary among the Jews. In so doing, Jesus revealed his intimate relationship with Father. Not everyone could (or would) refer to God as Father. This distinction made Jesus' relationship with God special and honoring. Jesus' reference to God as his Father revealed to the disciples who God was. The Israelites had viewed God as a distant sovereign from whom they kept their distance. Only priests, prophets and an occasional king dared draw close to him. For everyone else, He was that being who would destroy them if they drew too near. With Jesus' continual references to God as Father, he began to challenge any misconceptions the disciples had of him. When questioned about healing the lame man on the Sabbath, Jesus referred to how his Father operated. Jesus claimed to work in the same manner as his Father (John 5:17).

So that no one would mistake Jesus' use of "my Father" for an earthly father, he often specified his Father "in Heaven." He taught his disciples that those who acknowledged him before men, would be acknowledged before his Father in Heaven (Matthew 10:32-33). Jesus revealed to his disciples the heart of his Father in Heaven, that no children ("little ones") should perish (Matthew 18:14). To illustrate his followers' authority, Jesus told them that their agreement on earth would secure his Father in Heaven's response (Matthew 18:19). In order to impress them with the importance of forgiveness, Jesus warned them of his Father's response toward those who refuse to forgive (Matthew 18:35). Not only did Jesus identify his Father as being

God Addressed As Father

in Heaven, but he also identified him with the Kingdom being established on earth. At the Lord's Supper, Jesus informed his disciples that the next time he would drink the fruit of the vine was when they would do so together in Jesus' Father's kingdom (Matthew 26:29). Jesus' words imply a fulfillment of the Father's Kingdom established and fulfilled on earth rather than only in Heaven.

In prayer, Jesus specified who his Father was, eliminating any misunderstanding about whom he addressed. Also in prayer, Jesus identified his Father as Lord of Heaven and earth (Matthew 11:25-26; Luke 10:21). To the listening Jews, that could only mean Yahweh. Outside the tomb of Lazarus, Jesus once again addressed God as Father. The fact that Jesus called Lazarus from the tomb confirmed the Father-Son relationship he had with God (John 11:41-42). Not only did Jesus address God as Father, but he went further. He declared that all things and all authority had been handed over to him as son from the Father (Luke 10:22; Matthew 28:18). In Jesus' very personal prayer in the Garden of Gethsemane, he continued to refer to God as "my Father" (Matthew 26:39; Luke 22:42). Mark's gospel revealed an even more intimate relationship between Jesus and Father when Jesus referred to God as "Abba, Father" (Mark 14:36). On the cross, Jesus interceded on behalf of his executioners, asking his Father to forgive them (Luke 23:34). As Jesus' life expired, his final words were directed toward his Father, relinquishing his soul into his Father's hands (Luke 23:46). As a child, Jesus recognized God as his Father; again in death he acknowledged God as his Father.

At times, Jesus left off the identification of his Father as being in Heaven, and merely referred to God as "my Father" (Matthew 20:23; 25:34). However, with the abundance of occasions in which Jesus did specify exactly who his Father was, the added qualification was not necessary. On one occasion, Jesus revealed his Father as his willing protector. He told his disciples that he could appeal to his Father, who would send legions of angels to his aid (Matthew 26:53).

As he did in teaching the disciples to pray, Jesus alluded to the disciples' relationship with God as their Father. When he prepared the disciples for his departure, he delegated to them the authority that he had received from his Father (Luke 22:29). By doing this, Jesus strengthened his disciples' understanding that God was their Father as He was Jesus' Father. Preparing his disciples for his departure and the coming of the Holy Spirit, Jesus told his disciples that he was sending the promise of his Father (the Holy Spirit) (Luke 24:49). During Jesus' final prayer, offered up on behalf of his disciples and all believers, Jesus revealed their and our connection with Father.

During his prayer in John 17, Jesus made a key connection. He asked his Father to keep his followers in His name (John 17:11). Jesus said that he had made known Father's name to the disciples (John 17:24-26). The awareness of their new identity in God would be the foundation for living out Father's name in their own life. When Jesus taught the Lord's Prayer, he commanded the disciples to pray and declare the Father's name as hallowed (holy). Later in his John 17 prayer, Jesus identified each believer with the name of the Father and with him.

A Father gives his name

In life, there are few ways to receive a family name. A wife receives the name of her husband. Scripture reveals that believers - the church - are the bride of Jesus (Ephesians 5:25-27). Children born to a father also receive his name. John revealed that all who believe in Jesus receive the right to be called children of God (John 1:12). Implied in John's statement is the reality that they also receive Father's name. Finally, by adoption, an individual can receive a name. The apostle Paul

God Addressed As Father

used this imagery to reveal how men, born into sin through Adam, can be transformed and brought into God the Father's family (Romans 11:17-24).

Although the revelation of God as Father was not widely taught in the Old Testament, it was expressed. When God told Solomon that if His people, who are called by His name, would repent, He would heal their land. The fact that the people were called by God's name implied that He was their Father, who had given them His name (2 Chronicles 7:14). Furthermore, God described Himself as "Father" in His relationship with Solomon (2 Samuel 7:14). He is referred to as a "Father" in the sense that we are His creation, similar to Paul's reference in Acts 17:27-28 (Isaiah 64:8). He is called the Father of the people of Israel (Deuteronomy 32:6). The Messiah is entitled "Eternal Father" in Isaiah 9:6. Even with these references, the Jews refrained from praying to God as Father and were offended when Jesus called God "his Father".

Sometimes we gain glimpses of Kingdom relationships in cultural practices. In Italy, when a woman is married, she keeps her maiden name, but adds her husband's last name with the preposition, "in". For example, if my wife and I had been married in Italy instead of the United States, her name would have become Donelle Johnson in Freitag, rather than Donelle Freitag. When we become Christians, we do not change our name, even though our identity does change as we become children of God. However, the New Testament declares over ninety times that we are "in Christ." Being in Christ becomes part of our new identity and thus also our name, similar to the Italian custom. In this example, my wife, Donelle's name, would be "Donelle Freitag in Christ."

The sharing of Father's name reveals the believer's unity with Jesus and Father. Jesus interceded on behalf of the disciples regarding this unity (John 17:20-21). Between Jesus and Father

29

exist no relational barriers or secrets. Between them exist no grudges that hinder their communication. The relationship that Jesus and Father enjoy was to be the model for all relationships within the kingdom of God, including those between believers and Jesus and between all individual believers. This explains why, later in the Lord's Prayer, Jesus would place such a strong emphasis on forgiveness. Since no unforgiveness exists between the Father and the Son, then unforgiveness should not exist between believers.

Father gives us our purpose

In John's gospel, Jesus linked his mission as coming directly from his Father. To the Jews, Jesus clarified that God was his Father. Because they did not acknowledge Jesus as the Messiah, they revealed that they themselves did not belong to God, Jesus' Father. Jesus declared that he came in Father's name, meaning that he came with the full authority of Father, but the Jews rejected Jesus. Rather than acknowledging Jesus as God's Son, they preferred to give honor and glory to one another (John 5:43-44). With the people, Jesus revealed a misunderstanding. The people long believed that Moses had been the one to provide manna in the wilderness, but Jesus corrected their error. He revealed that it was his Father who provided the bread (manna) from Heaven, but also sent Jesus as the true bread who gave life to the world (John 6:32-33). Jesus went on to clarify that he was the bread of life, so that all who believed in him would receive eternal life from his Father and experience resurrection on the last day (John 6:35-40).

Upon confrontation with the Jews, Jesus bluntly revealed that God was his Father. Their attempt to seize Jesus revealed that they had understood him to be identifying God as his Father (John 8:19). As Jesus did that which he observed his Father doing, so also the Jews did that which they saw their father doing. Jesus revealed to them that they were deceived in their thinking. They believed that Abraham was their father and that they followed God, but Jesus declared that they were actually following the devil as their father (John 8:38-44).

Rather than accepting the truth of their actions, the Jews accused Jesus of having a demon. To this Jesus replied that he honored his Father, while they dishonored Jesus (John 8:49-51). Their confrontation escalated when Jesus declared that Abraham, whom they considered their father, had rejoiced to see the day when Jesus would walk the earth (John 8:54-56). The Jews could not accept this, because Jesus had not been alive during Abraham's lifetime over two thousand years prior. To this, Jesus gave his boldest declaration of being, not only Father's Son, but having the same sacred name as Father, when he declared to be "I AM" (John 8:58-59). The Jews grasped immediately what Jesus had done and tried to stone him to death, but Jesus escaped their efforts.

Because of Jesus' relationship with his Father, he had specific authority over life. Regarding his own life, Jesus declared that he had the authority to lay it down. No one else had the power or authority to take Jesus' life from him. On the cross, Jesus would reveal his authority when he committed his spirit into Father's hands (Luke 23:46; John 10:18). Jesus not only had authority over his own life, but he had the power to grant eternal life to those who followed him (John 10:25, 29). Those who believe in Jesus would reveal their connection to him by hearing his voice and then following him. Concluding his discourse with the Jews, Jesus challenged them to believe his claim based on the works that he did, which were the same works of God. Jesus' argument that he did as his Father did was one of the most convincing arguments for the Jews, bringing some, like Nicodemus, to belief in him (John 10:37; 3:2). As Jesus prepared himself and his disciples for his death, he drew comfort from his Father-Son relationship. Jesus revealed to the disciples that he was troubled with the prospect of his impending death; he even appealed to his Father to save him (John 12:27). However, Jesus drew strength from the fact that his death was the purpose of his life. To comfort to his disciples, Jesus reminded them of his connection with Father, which was applicable to them as well. Jesus reminded them that he was going to prepare an eternal dwelling for them in his Father's presence (John 14:2). His close connection with Father was revealed in his declaration to Philip that if they had seen Jesus, they had seen Father (John 14:7). By this, Jesus did not mean that he and Father were literally the same person. The disciples would not have arrived at that conclusion because, on more than one occasion, they had heard the voice of God the Father from Heaven, while in Jesus' presence. Rather, Jesus meant that through observing his life and works, they observed what Father desired to be done.

The arrival of the Holy Spirit would lift the disciples to another level of understanding the connection between Jesus and Father, because the Spirit would bring the disciples into a similar relationship (John 14:16-23). With the arrival of the Holy Spirit, dwelling forever with the individual believer in Jesus, both Jesus and Father would dwell with him (John 14:23). In this way, every individual believer would be a temple of God (1 Corinthians 6:20).

Jesus' Father would have an on-going role in each follower's life, shaping and preparing it so that it would produce fruit. By fruit, Jesus referred to the works that he did and that his followers would do in Father's name and in Jesus' name (John 15:1-8). Throughout his life, Jesus declared that he did the works of Father. In the same way, as Father and Son dwelt in the believer through the Holy Spirit, the believer would do Father's works as well. Jesus' followers would practice what Jesus taught and understand what Father desires (John 15:10-15). By their understanding, Jesus' followers revealed that they were no longer servants, but friends of Jesus. Through these words, Jesus revealed that he invited his disciples into a yet closer relationship with him and Father, because a friend enjoys a much closer relationship with the Master than does a servant. In effect, Jesus invited his disciples into a "first name" relationship with him.

After the resurrection, Jesus confirmed to Mary Magdalene, not only his connection with Father, but her's as well. As Mary clung to Jesus, he told her to cease, because he had not yet ascended to the Father (John 20:17). While it is unclear why Jesus instructed her to stop clinging to him because he had not yet ascended, it is clear that he identified God the Father as both his Father and her Father. Through Jesus, Mary and all believers are invited into a Father and child relationship, parallel and equivalent to what Jesus has.

Your Father

Even prior to Jesus' revelation of God as being Mary's Father, Jesus began to teach his disciples about their (our) Father in heaven. Consistently throughout the Gospels, Jesus referred to God as "your Father", when the expectation would be that he refer to God as "your God" or "your Lord." In so doing, Jesus stretched the disciples' concept of who God was to them.

When preparing his disciples for the conflict they would encounter, Jesus instructed them not to worry about how they would defend themselves before kings and governors. Jesus instructed them to be at peace because the Holy Spirit, the Spirit of their Father, would reveal to them what they must declare (Matthew 10:20). Because of the relationship and confidence in their Father, Jesus commanded his followers not to fear men, but to fear Father. While men could only destroy the human body through physical death, Father can destroy both body and soul in hell. However, Jesus added that it was not fear that was to motivate the disciples, but the knowledge that their heavenly Father knew every detail of their life and cared deeply about what happened to them (Matthew 10:28-31).

As Jesus' followers were not to live anxiously regarding what men could do to them, they were not to allow anxiety to enter their existence due to circumstances or fear of the future (Luke 12:30). While the people of this world seek to gain material or economic advantage in the world, Jesus' followers were not to live with such anxiety. Rather, they were to trust that their Father would provide exactly what they needed and when they needed it (Luke 12:30). In this way, the children of God the Father would reveal themselves to be radically distinct from the children of the world. Without worry hindering their life, children of Father could sell what they have and give generously to those in need, because they understood the vast resources they had from their Father in heaven. Children of Father's kingdom live in peace because they know that one day they will receive the entire kingdom into their hands (Luke 12:32). Since their heart is with their Father and not in the world, they have no need to acquire the possessions of the world (Luke 12:33-34).

The morning after driving out the merchants from the temple, Jesus instructed his disciples on faith and prayer. Jesus warned them regarding the devastating impact unforgiveness can have on their spiritual connection with their Father. Since their Father practiced forgiveness, they were to follow His example in order that their sins would be forgiven (Mark 11:25). Refusing to forgive others implies that they are not doing the works of their Father, but those of the devil. This was the warning that Jesus issued to the Jews who did not believe in him. Belief out of religious duty was never the connection with Jesus or Father, but living and doing the works of Father out of a childlike relationship with Him reveals the connection. In Luke, Jesus identified mercy as one of the defining characteristics of the disciples' Father. As His children, they were to be merciful as their Father is merciful. To not practice mercy was to reveal that they were not children of God the Father, but had another father who was never merciful (Luke 6:36).

Viewing Father differently

After all the specific teaching in the Gospels regarding God being the believer's Father as he was Jesus' Father, we would expect numerous references to God as "Father" in Acts. However, it seems like the believers hesitated to put this instruction into practice. Prior to his ascension into heaven, Jesus reinforced the concept of God being Father when he instructed the disciples that it was not time for them to know the times or epochs that Father had set (Acts 1:7). On that occasion, Jesus did not refer to God as his Father, or their Father, but due to Jesus' previous teaching and prayer in John 17, it was understood that God was Father to both. In his first sermon on the day of Pentecost, Peter maintained Jesus' terminology regarding God as Father. First, Peter spoke of what God had done, then he identified God as the Father who had sent the Holy Spirit to them (Acts 2:29-34). Peter subtly contrasted Jesus with David. Jesus had ascended into heaven and sent the Holy Spirit from Father, while David had died and remained in his tomb. Peter's example would have been powerful both in his contrast with Jesus, but also because the Jews tended to identify David with the Father of the Messiah. In so doing, Peter demonstrated both that Jesus was superior to David, Jesus' so-called Father, and that God himself was Jesus' Father.

Even though the first two chapters continued the concept of God as Father, the concept tended to shift shortly after. The church began to identify David as their father, similar to the Jews' view of David as "forefather" (Acts 4:25). Their declaration was a departure from the terminology that Jesus used. Although the Messiah was sometimes referred to as David's son, Jesus never referred to David as his father; rather

God Addressed As Father

Jesus implied that he was greater than David. Referring to David as father or forefather was a reflection of Jewish terminology but not Jesus' terminology. What is particularly ironic is that this declaration was done in prayer. The Jewish Christians had addressed their prayer to Lord, not as Father. Jesus had taught them that as his followers, God was their Father, but their prayer identified David as their father, not God. These references in prayer indicated that they were continuing to practice the Jewish views of God and David, rather than what Jesus had taught. Even so, we observe Father's mercy, because at the end of their prayer they were filled with the Holy Spirit. Our Father loves us so much that, even when we slip back into old ways of thinking He still identifies with us (Acts 4:31).

Some time later, Stephen would follow the example of the Christians when he declared Abraham to be their father (Acts 7:2). Again Stephen attempted to identify with his Jewish listeners because the Jews considered Abraham to be their father. However, Jesus had challenged the Jewish claim that Abraham was their father because they refused to acknowledge Jesus even though Abraham, himself, had looked forward to Jesus' day (John 8:39-59).

The early church's example of expressing a formal and distant relationship with Father in prayer was the first example of Christians expressing a servant relationship with Father rather than the intimate child one offered by Jesus. Today, many Christians have nothing more than a formal theological and religious relationship with Father. They are unaware that Jesus taught and offered a very different familial relationship that Father desires to have with them. This is something for us to consider. If our Father will pour out His boldness and power upon us even though we still persist in old ways of thinking, how much more will He pour out upon us when we grasp that we are His sons and daughters?

God Addressed As Father

We now promote the family business of Father's kingdom, promoted from being servants employed in the kingdom (John 15:15-16). While faithful servants are dedicated, beloved sons and daughters of a loving Father are much more dedicated and motivated to promote their Father's work and name. Paul described the struggle that we face as we work through the implications of being adopted sons. He reminded the Roman church that all of creation awaits the revelation of the sons of God (followers of Jesus); it even groans and suffers as in childbirth, waiting for our adoption as sons and the redemption of our body (Romans 8:18-22). Jesus said that those who believed in him would do greater works than those he had done (John 14:12). It may be that we need to work out the implication of our being sons and daughters before we can fully understand what Jesus spoke.

While the early church seemed to stray, some from Jesus' instruction to address God as Father, Paul, in his writings, often referred to God as "our Father." To the believers, Paul began each of his letters declaring grace and peace to them from "God our Father" and the "Lord Jesus Christ" (Romans 1:7; 1 Corinthians 1:3; 2 Corinthians 1:2-3; Galatians 1:1-3; Ephesians 1:2-3; 6:23; Philippians 1:2; Colossians 1:2-3; 1 Thessalonians 1:1; 2 Thessalonians 1:1-2; 1 Timothy 1:2; 2 Timothy 1:2; Titus 1:4; Philemon 1:3). Paul's consistency in every one of his letters underscored his belief that God was to be viewed as Father, while Jesus was identified as either Lord or Savior. What is powerful in Paul's example is that he was thoroughly trained in Judaism, yet he did not allow his training from youth to distract him from what Jesus revealed about the relationship that he and all believers enjoyed with God as Father.

In Romans, Paul referred to both Abraham and God as "father." Although Paul addressed God as "our Father" (Romans 1:7) and Abraham as "our father" (Romans 4:12), it is clear that Paul referred to them in a different sense. While God is our

God Addressed As Father

heavenly Father, Paul referred to Abraham as our spiritual father (Romans 4:16-17). Abraham became our spiritual father because he trusted God and therefore paved the way for all who come to God through faith in Jesus. Because Father calls us into a father-like relationship with him, Paul referred to Abraham as one who set an example of faith that we are called to follow.

Even though Paul came to faith after Jesus' life, resurrection and ascension, he identified the intimate relationship that the believer enjoys with God the Father. We, through a faith like Abraham's, have been adopted into Father's family, making Him not only our Father, which is more formal, but our Abba (papa or daddy) (Romans 8:15; Galatians 4:6). It is interesting that in the Gospels there is only one instance of Jesus referring to God as "Abba Father" (Mark 14: 13). In the midst of his pain, Jesus related to God as a small child would to his Father. We have no example of Jesus ever teaching the disciples to address God in this manner; only did he teach "Father." However, Paul revealed in both Romans 8 and Galatians 4, that the Holy Spirit prompts us to address Father with that same childlike address. In this way, we begin to fulfill what Jesus taught, that unless we become like children, we will never enter the Kingdom of God.

Our close relationship with Father is confirmed because of the presence of the Holy Spirit dwelling in our lives. As Jesus had prophesied to his followers, the Holy Spirit is the one who instructs us to refer to God as Father. By both Jesus and Paul's use of the title, Abba, for God, we understand that God calls us to an affectionate and intimate relationship with Him through Jesus. A small child would call his father "papa" or "daddy," so we believers in Jesus call on our Father in the same manner. To the Corinthians, Paul declared that there were not multiple gods, as the Roman pagan religion taught, but there was only one Lord, Jesus, and one God, our Father (1 Corinthians 8:6). Several times in prayer, Paul asked that knowledge and wisdom be granted to know the Father of glory (Ephesians 1:17; 3:14;

God Addressed As Father

Philippians 2:11; Colossians 1:12; 1 Thessalonians 3:11-13; 2 Thessalonians 2:16-17). Paul was asking our heavenly Father to give us the ability to know him more deeply. He explained that through Jesus, we now have full access to Father through the ministry of the Holy Spirit in our lives (Ephesians 2:18). Father is over all and in all through the active presence of the Holy Spirit (Ephesians 4:6). Since we have such a close relationship with Father, we are called to give Him thanks (Philippians 4:20; Colossians 3:17; 1 Thessalonians 1:2-3).

In Paul's letters, several themes emerge. He began each of his letters extending grace and peace to the recipients from God the Father and the Lord or Savior Jesus. While Jesus' relationship with us could be called either Lord or Savior, God's was always Father. In numerous letters, Paul expressed a desire that the believer recognize Father's glory through an increased knowledge of Him. Finally, since we've been gifted with increased knowledge of Father through the Spirit, we are to continually give thanks to Him.

Summary

Jesus challenged and changed two thousand years of Jewish history when he declared God to be his Father. Abraham at best viewed God as his friend. To Moses, God revealed His name as "Yahweh," meaning "I AM." David and the other prophets related to Him as Lord. The Jews were so hesitant in addressing God that they would not even pronounce His name, continuing to refer to Him as Lord, or Adonai in Hebrew. Nowhere in the Old Testament are the Jews found praying to God as Father.

When Jesus affirmed his Son relationship with God by referring to Him as Father, the Jews were not only offended, but they used his action as another reason to plot against him. They understood Jesus' actions as making him equal to God. While an example of the Messiah being God's son could be found in the

God Addressed As Father

Old Testament, the concept of Messiah's followers calling God "Father" was unprecedented. Yet, that is exactly what Jesus taught his followers to do. He taught them about God, "your Father." He taught them to pray to "Our Father." In so doing, Jesus subjected his disciples to the same accusation which was made against him, that they were making themselves equal to God. Jesus' instruction reveals the radical teaching that he gave to his followers.

While the early church seemed to back away from identifying God as Father in prayer, preferring to identify Him as Lord, surprisingly Paul, the educated Jew, understood the Father – Son relationship that the believer enjoyed with God. Paul reiterated what Jesus had taught, that the believer could approach God not only in a more formal manner as "Father," but also in an intimate manner as "papa" or "daddy." In every one of Paul's letters, he referred to God as Father, even though he would change how he referred to Jesus. His consistency emphasized his understanding of his relationship with God.

Most of us, if ever invited into the powerful atmosphere of the Oval Office, would hesitate to bring our young children (or grandchildren). If we did dare to bring small children, propriety would dictate that we require them to sit quietly before the President. However, there is a photograph taken in the early 1960's of President Kennedy in the Oval Office with his two children, Carolyn and John Jr. What is he doing? He is sitting in a chair to the right of his desk, clapping as his children skip and dance before him. You see, if daddy is President, its OK to dance and skip in the Oval Office. This photograph gives us a glimpse of our relationship with Abba Father. As believers, we need to grasp the fact that our Abba (Daddy) in heaven delights over us in a similar manner (Zephaniah 3:17).

God Addressed As Father

Questions for Reflection

1. When you pray, to whom do you usually pray (Father, Jesus, Holy Spirit)?

2. When talking to Father what specific title(s) do you employ?

3. How do your references in prayer reveal your intimacy with Father, Jesus and the Holy Spirit?

4. How does Father's delight over you as His child impact your relationship with Him?

Our Papa in heaven, we thank you for opening the way for us to enter into such a close and affectionate relationship with you. We acknowledge that your great love for us as your children surpasses even the love and kindness of the best of our human fathers. Teach us to grow in our knowledge of your affection, love and commitment to us, so that we may reflect your love back to you. Amen.

Declaring God's Name Holy

The creation must declare God's glory. We men have a choice; nevertheless it is our created purpose to declare God's holiness. When the Pharisees told Jesus to keep the people from praising him, Jesus responded that if they did not give praise, the rocks would cry out (Luke 19:39-40). The Psalms declare that God will be exalted among the nations (Psalm 46:10). If the inanimate creation along with the nations must declare the holiness of God, then certainly His people must do so in prayer. God is holy; therefore it is our purpose to declare His holiness. If we refuse to declare God's holiness continually, we deny our identity as men, choosing to live as less than men, for purposes that are beneath who we are.

Name meaning

In the New Testament, a person's name reflected who he was, declaring his character and being. Today a name is merely a means of identification. Biblically, a name declares who a person is, not only what he or she is called. In the Bible, when a father named his child, he made a prophetic declaration of who that child would become. Other times, his naming described what he saw the child to be. When Isaac named his sons, he named Esau (red), because that was his son's complexion. He gave the name "Jacob" (grasper) to his second son, because at birth he was grasping the heal of Esau. In Jacob's case, his name also implied deceiver, which is what Jacob became. God's name also declares who he is. Declaring God's name to be holy is the same as declaring God to be holy. That means that as we examine the names of God we discover who he is as well.

Jesus' Name: Salvation

When Gabriel appeared to Joseph, Mary's husband-to-be, he declared the name of Mary's baby, Jesus (Matthew 1:21). Jesus was named from heaven to declare who he was as Savior.

45

Declaring God's Name Holy

Unfortunately, the English name "Jesus" may cause us to miss the original meaning of Jesus' name. We get the name "Jesus" through ancient Greek "Iesus." Then it was translated into Latin "Iesu," from which we derive the name "Jesus" in English. However, Jesus' name in Hebrew was "Yeshua," from which we derive the English name "Joshua." Originally the name "Yeshua" came from two Hebrew words "Yahweh," the name God revealed to Moses at the burning bush (Exodus 3:14) and "yasha" the Hebrew verb meaning "to save." The resultant meaning was "the LORD (Yahweh) saves." In other words, when Gabriel revealed Mary's son's name, his name declared him to be "savior."

Jesus' name declares that he was more than what men typically declare him to be. Jesus asked his disciples who the people said that he was. In response, they said that the people declared Jesus to be Elijah, a prophet, or John the Baptist. It is true that Jesus was a prophet, but his name declared that he was more than a prophet. Jesus' name prevented him from being anything less than Savior and Messiah. If he had been a prophet, even one as great as Elijah, who was prophesied to come, he would not have been Savior. A prophet could not be Savior; he had to be the Messiah.

The rest of the New Testament makes astounding affirmations related to the name of Jesus. Since Jesus is Savior, God the Father declares us to be righteous, or justified, in relationship to His Law in the name of Jesus (1 Corinthians 6:11; 1 John 2:12). Jesus fulfilled the law perfectly as well as having received the condemnation of the law as if he had broken it. His dual feat of fulfilling the law and enduring its condemnation makes him unique among men and able to offer justification for all who appeal to him. As such, Jesus is the only one in whose name everyone is invited to come to receive forgiveness and rest for his soul (Matthew 11:28-30; Acts 4:12).

Declaring God's Name Holy

Although Jesus is not universally recognized as Savior and the rightful ruler of the universe, someday he will be. There will come a day, when, by bowing before his name, all men who have ever lived will recognize Jesus for who he is (Philippians 2:9, 10). In ancient Babylon, Nebuchadnezzar built a statue before which all the people had to bow in order to recognize him (Daniel 3:4-5). What Nebuchadnezzar forced his people to do because of his pride, people will naturally and rightfully do before Jesus, because all authority in heaven and on earth has been given to him.

God's forgiveness of sin comes through only one means, repentance. However, repentance is more than an acknowledgment of wrongdoing. Everyday, people show up in recovery group meetings, declaring that they were wrong in their addictions; yet, that repentance does not lead to forgiveness and reconciliation with God. It also does not lead to their being free from their addition. Merely acknowledging our sin does not lead to forgiveness; rather it can lead to death. Consider Judas, who "repented," only to go out and commit suicide. What is needed is a repentance that leads to God's forgiveness, rather than to sorrow and death (2 Corinthians 2:10). On Pentecost, the Jews of Jerusalem responded to Peter by asking what they must do. Peter told them to repent, but to do so in the name of Jesus (Acts 2:38). That day, three thousand were added to the kingdom of God. This was not through mere acknowledgment of sin, but acknowledgment of Jesus' name that led to forgiveness and life change. Repentance and belief is a declaration of Jesus' name as Savior. In the Lord's Prayer, God's name is declared holy. As we place our trust in Jesus and repent from past sins, we declare Jesus' name to be Savior.

What Peter did on the day of Pentecost was apply what Jesus said must be done throughout the whole world. On the night of Jesus' resurrection, Jesus reminded his disciples that repentance for the forgiveness of sins would be proclaimed in

Declaring God's Name Holy

His name (Luke 24:47). What does this mean? It refers to authority. It is with Jesus' authority that his followers go out into all the world and proclaim the forgiveness of sins, because only God, not man, can forgive sins.

The Jews understood that only God could forgive sins; that is why they had an issue with Jesus (Mark 2:6-7). They were correct. Only God can forgive sins, but they were wrong in their understanding because they failed to recognize Jesus as the Messiah, God, who came in flesh (John 1:14). When Jesus' followers go out into the world, they do so under the power and presence of the Holy Spirit, the Spirit of Jesus in their life. The Holy Spirit, being the Spirit of Jesus, has all authority, including authority over sickness, the demonic, nature, death and the authority to forgive sins. As Jesus' followers go out into the world and declare salvation in Jesus' name, they are declaring who Jesus is. On the contrary, when followers of Jesus deny the authority of Jesus' name, in effect they deny the power and authority of the Holy Spirit who has taken up residence in their life (2 Timothy 3:5). Quite possibly they have accepted a lie that Satan has suggested to them in order to keep them trapped in a weak and powerless spiritual condition. Trapped in that condition, they believe that they will always remain struggling with the same difficulties in their life instead of experiencing the victory for which Jesus died (Romans 8:37).

Having repented in Jesus' name and received the forgiveness of sins, Jesus' followers become children of God in Jesus' name (John 1:12). Repentance in his name leads to a completely new identity for the Jesus-follower. In a sense, they cease even being human as the world defines it. Natural man is a descendant of Adam; therefore, he is in prison to his sinful desires. He is a member of Adam's family. Those who repent in Jesus' name are adopted into a new family and become part of a new race of which Jesus is the head (Romans 5:12-21; 1 Corinthians 15:20-26). The Bible teaches that there is only one name through

48

which we can receive eternal life, Jesus' name (Acts 4:12). It is significant that Luke did not say believing in Jesus gives eternal life, but believing in Jesus' name. In other words, believing in Jesus' name is the same as believing in Jesus, the person. As we believe and receive eternal life, we also declare Jesus' name to be salvation.

Prayer

Jesus made extraordinary promises to those who come to Father in Jesus' name. He will do whatever we ask (John 14:13, 14). Jesus called us to bear fruit, therefore, He will do what we ask in His name (John 15:16). Prior to Jesus' instruction, the disciples had not prayed to Father in Jesus' name. Jesus introduced this concept during the Last Supper. In fact, when Jesus taught them to pray with what is called the Lord's Prayer, he didn't mention anything about praying in his name, but in John 14, 15, and 16, Jesus introduced his disciples to addressing Father as though they were Jesus himself, "in his name" (John 16:23, 24, 26).

When we reflect upon Jesus' words, his statement is outrageous. Jesus' teaching in the Lord's prayer implies that we are to address God the Father in exactly the same way that he does. We can enter into the throne room of heaven and address Father as though we were Jesus himself (Hebrews 4:16). Furthermore, Father responds to us as if we were indeed Jesus. Jesus took our place by being condemned for our sin; we join him before Father's throne in prayer. With these words, Jesus implies to us that we can enter into the Father's presence with confidence that Father will hear us and respond. As we never see one example of Jesus pleading with the Father or begging Him in prayer, this type of address to Father is also inappropriate for us.

Declaring God's Name Holy

Identification

When I studied Italian in Florence, Italy, a Roman Catholic children's hospital was pointed out to me. In centuries past, people would anonymously leave children there. Those children were left without a name or knowledge of their past. They were cut off from their history. This is what Scripture says happened to us. The priests and nuns took in abandoned children and gave them a home; God did that and more for us. The priests and nuns could not give the children a family name and history, but God applied to us His own name through marriage (Ezekiel 16:8-14) and claimed us for His own. Paul picked up the same concept in Ephesians, when he reminded his readers that as Gentiles, they had no means to approach God. However, through Jesus' blood, we are brought near. We have been identified with the name of Jesus and received Father's own name, which in prayer we declare to be hallowed and holy (Ephesians 2:11-13). In other words, when we declare Father's name to be holy, that declaration reflects back on our own identity as his children who have also received His name.

Beginning in the Old Testament, an amazing truth was revealed. God's people would be identified with His name. God revealed to Solomon that when His people, called by His name, would pray and humble themselves He would heal their land (2 Chronicles 7:14). In that revelation, God revealed to Solomon the intimate relationship He would have with His people, even when they were disobedient. God's people would gain their identity from His name in the same way a wife would take her husband's name; and in the same way that children, even adopted children, would receive the name of their father.

Centuries later, during the time of the prophet Isaiah, God would again identify his people as having "His name" (Isaiah 43:7). In the context, Isaiah was expressing God's comfort to His people so that they would not live in fear, but know that they

Declaring God's Name Holy

have been redeemed and are precious in His sight (Isaiah 43:1-4). Even more surprising were Amos' words. While 2 Chronicles 7:14 and Isaiah 43:7 would naturally be understood as identifying Jews with God's name, Amos declared that the nations (Gentiles) would also be included in God's name (Amos 9:12). Through his prophets, God revealed that His family would include not only Jews, but peoples from every tribe, tongue, people and nation (Revelation 5:9). In the New Testament, all believers' identity became associated with Jesus and Father's identity.

When the disciples observed another casting out demons in Jesus' name, questions were raised. The disciples' observation reveals that others, who were not among the twelve, also had received the authority to cast out demons in Jesus' name. The disciples were shocked, because apparently they thought that they had the exclusive responsibility of casting out demons in Jesus' name. They took matters into their own hands and tried to stop the man doing such things. However, Jesus corrected his disciples, informing them that anyone operating with his authority in his name will not work against himself and the kingdom (Mark 9:38, 39, 41; Luke 9:49). This account reveals a remarkable power associated with Jesus' name. Apparently this man, or men, had not received a directive from Jesus to cast out demons in Jesus' name, yet he did so with success. Quite likely, this man understood the implications of what he had heard Jesus teach, just like the Centurion had surmised that Jesus, because of his authority, could heal his servant without actually being present (Matthew 8:8-11).

This man had probably observed Jesus casting out demons and healing people. Perhaps he had also observed Jesus' disciples doing the same in Jesus name, so that he perceived it was not the disciples' power, but the authority of Jesus' name by which demons were cast out. By imitating what Jesus and his disciples did, this man confirmed the power that Jesus' name carried. So much so that his actions disturbed Jesus' disciples who assumed this power was reserved for their small group.

Not only are men identified with the name of Jesus, but the Holy Spirit's presence in the world is also connected to Jesus. During the Last Supper, Jesus taught his twelve followers that the Holy Spirit would come in Jesus' name (John 14:26). Jesus declared that Father would send the Holy Spirit, not in Father's name, but in Jesus' name.

Because of the Holy Spirit with us, we know that Jesus' presence is always near, but when more than one believer is gathered, then Jesus comes in a unique manner (Matthew 18:20). The context of the church making a decision together implies that this unique authority is granted when believers gather together and come into agreement. On several occasions, Scripture emphasized the importance of believers being like-minded (Romans 15:5; Philippians 2:2, 20). When believers gather together and make a united decision, the Holy Spirit grants a particular authority and power to that decision. These examples encourage believers to gather together, coming to united decisions for the advancement of the Kingdom of God. Perhaps the fractured nature of local churches is one reason that transforming power is lacking within many modern, western churches.

Jesus' name further impacts the way that we treat one another. We are to receive one another in Jesus' name. In other words, we are to treat others as if they were Jesus himself. How we think about and speak to one another is to be governed by considering them to be Jesus himself (Matthew 18:5). Since Jesus, in the person of the Holy Spirit, is present with every believer, then it follows that we should treat them as we would treat Jesus. Not treating someone with the same respect, honor and dignity that we would give to Jesus, in effect denies the presence and person of the Holy Spirit in that person. Our lack of respect for a person implies that we don't acknowledge that the person is in Christ and belongs to him. John instructed the church that the name of Jesus fuels our love for one another (1 John 3:23). If the love of Jesus is in us, then we will love others; not doing so denies the presence of the Holy Spirit in our own life. Not only are our relationships to be governed by the name of Jesus, but all of our actions come under the authority of Jesus' name (Colossians 3:17). Finally, Jesus' name deserves glory. As believers give honor to one another, Jesus' name is also glorified (2 Thessalonians 1:12).

Several years ago, I remember riding in the car with my sister, whose husband was an officer in the Air Force. When we drove onto the base, the guard saluted her. I asked her why. She explained that their car had a sticker that identified its owner as an officer. The enlisted man saluted the authority that was associated with the car, even though not one of us within the car were in the Air Force. Since Jesus has identified us with his name, we are to treat one another with the same respect and dignity that Jesus' name requires.

Authority

Our identification with Jesus means that every believer possesses a certain amount of authority. Those who followed Jesus were given authority over the opposing spiritual forces in this world. During Jesus' lifetime his followers (the seventy) went out and cast out demons in Jesus' name (Luke 10:17).

After the coming of the Holy Spirit believers confirmed what Jesus said in Mark 16:17 about his followers doing signs and wonders in his name (Acts 4:30; 16:18; 19:13, 17). What Jesus did, he taught his followers to do. The apostles modeled the authority associated with Jesus' name, then ordinary believers like Stephen and Philip revealed that any ordinary believer has authority in Jesus' name (Acts 6:8; 8:6; James 5:16-18). Jesus left us, not as orphans, but as children who have rights and authority (John 1:12; Hebrews 4:16). He has not left us to live in fear and timidity, but has given us his Spirit so that we can live life like he modeled for us, with power, love, discipline and authority (John 14:18; Romans 1:16; 2 Timothy 1:7). The way we pray, declaring the name of God to be holy, and the confidence with which we live our lives, will reveal what we believe about our relationship with Jesus. Our prayers should reflect that we are children of God with privilege and rights, and not guests, visitors or strangers in his house.

Suffering

Although in Jesus' name we receive salvation, new identification and authority, Jesus gave his disciples warning. In the United States, we assume that anyone fully committed to following Jesus will benefit from the American dream of affluence and comfort. However following Jesus also means that we could experience hatred from society (Matthew 10:22; 24:9). After reflection, what Jesus taught his disciples makes perfect sense, because even though Jesus lived fully identified with the Father and operated according to the power of the Holy Spirit, men who were committed to religion hated him. Even more surprising is that close family and friends will turn against those committed to living under the authority of Jesus and the Holy Spirit (Luke 21:16).

The plots of the Jewish ruling council against Paul, a former friend and colleague, illustrates the potential conflict experienced by those identified with Jesus' name. A life-changing commitment to Jesus is always a threat to those who merely want to follow Jesus as a religion. Yet, despite the difficulty faced in life, Jesus gave an extraordinary promise. This promise was that not one hair on their heads would perish because their enduring commitment to Jesus would provide them with life. Jesus promised his disciples that whatever sacrifice they made in his name would be recognized (Matthew 19:29; Luke 21:17-18).

So that we do not fail to comprehend what Jesus taught, the book of Acts confirmed what Jesus declared. The disciples lived with great power and authority, but they also suffered for it, mainly from those committed to maintaining religious traditions. Because the apostles would not stop proclaiming the resurrection, the Jewish leaders beat them. Amazingly, the apostles rejoiced because they were considered worthy to suffer in Jesus' name (Acts 5:41; 1 Peter 4:14). The life-transforming power of the gospel is revealed again through the unusual response to suffering, revealed in the lives of Christians. Jesus described Paul as the one who would bear his name before the nations and suffer much for Jesus' sake (Acts 9:15-16). Toward the end of his life, Paul went to Jerusalem having been prophetically warned that he would endure suffering for the name of Jesus (Acts 21:13).

Not only do Jesus' true disciples operate in the authority and power of his name, but some will come in Jesus' name with the purpose of deceiving many. They come in Jesus' name, pretending to be Jesus. Unfortunately, many will fall for their lie and be misled (Matthew 24:4-5). However, Jesus told his disciples in advance so that they would not be misled and would be ready for those who told lies (Matthew 24:25-26).

Implied in biblical teaching regarding Jesus' name is that as a believer follows Jesus, by his life he declares the Father's name "holy." Not only does he declare the Father's name to be holy in prayer, but his actions reflect the holiness and power associated with him through Jesus.

The Father's Name

Jesus became flesh and lived in Father's name, so followers of Jesus go out in Jesus' name. As Jesus revealed the Father to us, followers of Jesus reveal him to the world through their life filled by the Holy Spirit. When Jesus entered into Jerusalem on Palm Sunday, just a few days before his crucifixion, the crowds recognized him as coming in the name of the LORD (Matthew 21:9; Mark 11:9-10; Luke 19:38; John 12:13). A few days later, Jesus wept over what he saw coming upon Jerusalem, declaring that the next time he would come, they would recognize him as the one coming in the name of the Father (Matthew 23:39; Luke 13:35).

In the face of conflict and challenge, Jesus defended his authority to heal on the Sabbath because he came in Father's name (John 5:43). As our authority to operate in Jesus' name is delegated to us, Jesus also operated with delegated authority from Father. When the Jewish leaders questioned Jesus' validity as a teacher, Jesus reminded them that His works demonstrated that He had come in the name of the Father (John 10:25).

One of Jesus' purposes in becoming flesh was for him to reveal the nature of Father. While praying to Father, Jesus stated that he had revealed Father's name to his followers (John 17:6, 25-26). At that same time, Jesus declared the name of Father, rather than our vision or theology, to be the basis of Christian's unity (John 17:11-12). So that we do not misunderstand, Jesus clarified later, saying that he not only prayed for the twelve, but also all those who would ever believe because of the testimony of the twelve (John 17:20).

Not only did Jesus reveal Father's name, but Jesus' ministry was the fulfillment of what the Old Testament declared about his ministry. David declared that Father's name would be declared through the Messiah (Psalm 22:22 quoted in Hebrews 2:12). As

Declaring God's Name Holy

every believer follows Jesus in the power of the Holy Spirit,
Jesus reveals to him or her the name of Father, and the Father
himself. It should not surprise us that Jesus taught us to pray by
declaring Father's name to be holy. Father's will is for His name
to be declared throughout the whole earth.

Interestingly, Scripture declares that God raised up Pharaoh
so that His name would be proclaimed to all people for the whole
earth had heard about the plagues and protected the Jewish
people by passing them through the Red Sea. Knowledge of
what God did caused peoples all over the world to fear the Jews,
because He was the Jews' God (Exodus 9:16 quoted in Romans
9:17). Each time they heard what God had done, His name was
revealed as holy.

David prophesied that the Gentiles would know God
because God's name was praised (Psalm 18:49 quoted in Romans
15:9). As followers of Jesus praise the name of the Father, those
who don't know him (Gentiles) will hear of the holiness of
Father's name. It is Father's heart to form a people for this name
out of all the nations of the earth (Acts 15:14).

Paul instructed slaves to honor their earthly masters so that
the name of Father would not be dishonored (blasphemed) (1
Timothy 6:1). James warned the rich to change their lifestyle,
because they were blaspheming the name of the Father (James
2:6-7). As we give praise to Father, even sacrificing in order to
praise, we give thanks to Father's name (Hebrews 13:15). Not
only are we to declare the name of Father as holy, but through
our actions declare Him holy as well.

Hallowed

As we've already seen, the concept of a name is extremely
important in the Bible. The name of Jesus and the name of the
Father are equivalent to Jesus and the Father. Jesus taught us to

Declaring God's Name Holy

declare the name of Father as "hallowed." The word, "hallowed," means to make something holy or to sanctify something, literally to set something apart for God's possession and use. The name of God is His name and therefore His unique possession; it belongs to Him alone. The word, "hallowed," is often translated as "sanctified." We are instructed to set certain things apart to be sanctified or holy in our lives.

To sanctify something means to reserve it for only one use. For example, when someone is employed for a company, he is given access to information that is to be reserved only for that corporation. Typically companies require their employees to sign a confidentiality agreement, declaring that they will not divulge private information outside the confines of work. In other words, the information is holy or sanctified to the corporation. While we don't typically use the terms holy, or sanctified, in reference to work information because of the religious connotations, that is what they are. When we refer to the name of Father as holy, or ourselves as holy, that means that Father's name and we ourselves are to be reserved only for Kingdom purposes.

As we declare the name of Father as holy, hallowed, or sanctified, other things happen in our life. We sanctify Jesus in our hearts (1 Peter 3:15). As we sanctify Jesus, we are always to be ready to explain to those who may ask why we have hope in this life despite the difficulties that we face. It is our hope in Jesus that declares Jesus to be holy in our hearts. As we declare Father's name to be holy in prayer, we are also sanctifying Jesus in our hearts.

Christians sanctified

Not only are Father's name and Jesus himself sanctified, but Father sanctifies us as followers of Jesus through the power of his truth (John 17:17). As he gave a farewell address to the Ephesian leaders, Paul declared that all who are sanctified belong to Father and His grace (Acts 20:32). In declaring this message to the Ephesian leaders, Paul summarized the message that he had received from Jesus at his conversion. Jesus revealed to Paul that his life mission was to proclaim forgiveness to the nations, freeing them from the dominion of Satan through being sanctified by faith in Jesus himself (Acts 26:15-18). As Jesus revealed to Paul, our sanctification comes through faith; it is accomplished through the power of the Holy Spirit operating in an individual's life (1 Corinthians 6:11). It is not just our spiritual life that is sanctified, but also our body and soul (1 Thessalonians 5:23). Jesus brings complete transformation to our whole being, not just a part of us.

Our sanctification is not for ourselves; Jesus sanctifies us through His death for a purpose (Hebrews 2:11; 10:10, 14). Paul reminded us that believers are transformed and rendered holy for the purpose of accomplishing good works in the kingdom of God (2 Timothy 2:21). Since the Christian's sanctification came at the price of Jesus' life, a Christian is to treat Jesus' death with respect and honor (Hebrews 10:29). Therefore the Christian is to live his life in a manner worthy of what it cost Jesus to purchase and sanctify it (Revelation 22:11).

Summary

In the Lord's Prayer's first command/declaration, the foundation for our Christian life is illustrated. We declare God's name to be hallowed, or holy and sanctified. It is God's own personal name which reveals His character. In his declaration, every follower of Jesus Christ associates himself with God's holy name through Jesus. The indwelling presence of the Holy Spirit in the believer's life reminds the individual of his new identity with Jesus and thus with the Father's holy name as well. In his new identity, he lives in the same power and authority that Jesus had according to the promises Jesus has given to him.

For each of us as followers of Jesus, we gain our identity through Father's name as his children (John 1:12). That name we declare to be holy. As the bride of Jesus, we derive our authority and power as we fulfill our commission to make disciples in his name (Matthew 28:18-20).

Questions for Reflection

1. How does your new identity in Christ, as one who is identified with God's name, impact the way that you view yourself and your life?

2. Since you are holy and set apart for the exclusive purposes of Father, how does that truth impact your daily decisions?

3. How might continually declaring God's name to be holy impact your thoughts, family and daily life?

Papa, you are completely unique, set apart and holy. I thank you because your holy and hallowed name has been given to me as your child. I declare you to be holy in my life and in my world so that your holiness may transform the atmosphere in which I live and breathe. May the reason why the angels forever and ever cry holy, be made further known to me that I may declare it to those I meet. Amen.

Chapter 4
Declaring God's Kingdom
Matthew 6:10

One aspect that makes the United States unique is the fact that, for over two hundred years, we've had a means of successfully transferring the authority to rule from one man to another. Our constitution clearly delineates the succession of power, normally through an election followed by an inauguration. In those times when a president died in office or the four times when a president was assassinated, the Vice-President has been sworn in to take his place. When President Nixon resigned, Gerald Ford, even though he was an appointed, not elected Vice-President, was sworn in as our Thirty-Eighth President. In any nation where it is not clear who has the right to rule, confusion reigns, because people in any organization want to know who is in charge and making decisions. The same is true in the Kingdom of God.

The second declaration Jesus commanded his followers to make in prayer was to affirm back to Father the coming of His Kingdom. The term, "kingdom," can be understood in several senses. First, "kingdom" can refer to the authority of a king to rule. In this sense, "kingdom" refers to the legitimacy of a person's ruling authority. Some rule because they have taken power by force and have removed the legitimate ruler, but they rule with usurped power which is not a legal rule. The second way the word, "kingdom" can be understood is a realm. This refers to the area over which the ruler is sovereign. When a legitimate ruler does in fact rule over the land which he or she is responsible, then that geographic region is his or her kingdom. Queen Elizabeth II is queen over Britain and the British Commonwealth. They are her "realm." However, she has no authority in the United States, because the USA is not part of her kingdom or realm. Jesus is the legitimate ruler over all creation; according to Matthew 28:18, all authority in Heaven and earth has been given to him. Even though right now, Jesus is the King

Declaring God's Kingdom

of kings and Lord of lords in Heaven, there is significant opposition to his rule on earth. In a sense, Jesus has a type of government in exile in Heaven, as his Kingdom is declared, established and expanded on earth. When Jesus declared that he would build his church and the gates of Hades would not be able to stand against it, he implied the growing nature of his Kingdom on earth (Matthew 16:18).

Father declared the growing and expanding nature of Jesus' kingdom in Psalm 110:1, when He declared to the Son to sit at His right hand until He made Jesus' enemies a footstool. Part of Father's making Jesus' enemies a footstool is through the prayer declarations of Jesus' followers declaring God's Kingdom, which will be governed by Jesus to be reality now on earth.

In May and June of 1940, the Nazi's went around the French line of defense by invading Holland and Belgium. Rather than attacking France from the east, where France had built defenses, they poured in from the north. To defeat France, the Nazi's first defeated France's weaker allies, Belgium and Holland, so that they could attack its undefended northern border. The Nazis drove the French army, along with the British Expeditionary force, into the coastal city of Dunkirk. Boats and ships of all shapes and sizes evacuated the troops so that they could go to England and prepare to fight another day. Shortly after the French and British evacuation, the Germans took Paris and the French officially surrendered on June 22, 1940. However, some French leaders made it to England and set up a free French government in Britain. The Allies considered this government the legitimate government of France, but it could not rule from France itself. It was called a government in exile. Yet in France, there were still Frenchmen, who lived their normal daily lives, but fought to restore a democratic government to France. They appeared to be normal citizens, but with great sacrifice, they fought for the freedom and re-establishment of a democratic French government. They fought until the Allies would send an

Declaring God's Kingdom

invasion force into France and complete the restoration of a democratic France. Four years after the evacuation at Dunkirk, on June 6, 1944, the Allies invaded France at Normandy. A little over a year after that, in July 1945, the Nazis surrendered and the war was over. France was once again democratic.

I tell you this, because in a sense, we, followers of Jesus, are like those citizens of France, laboring for the re-establishment of a democratic France. Jesus is the legitimate King of kings and Lord of lords upon the earth; however much of the earth does not recognize his leadership. You and I, as his followers, work to expand his kingdom on earth, not through assault rifles and bombs, but through powerful declarations that carry the power and authority of Jesus himself. One day, however, Jesus will return and take his rightful place as the ruler of this world. In the meantime we expand the kingdom here.

Kingdom proclaimed

Communication is essential in establishing a kingdom and a right to rule. During elections, people watch their televisions, seeking to know who will be their next legitimate ruler. During a coup attempt, rebels fight to obtain a means of communication, specifically television or radio stations, so that they can broadcast their message to the nation. At the same time, governments try to protect those means of communication. Governments and rebels both know that those who control the means of communication possess a great power over the nation, because people are influenced by the message that they hear.

In the case of Jesus, Father raised up and sent out John the Baptist to prepare His people for the Kingdom of Heaven's coming. One of the central messages of John's ministry was that the Kingdom of Heaven was at hand (Matthew 3:2; Mark 1:14-15). John's message implied that the Kingdom was not yet

Declaring God's Kingdom

present on earth, but it was coming, therefore, the people were to prepare for it through repentance. Even after he revealed himself as the Messiah, Jesus announced the same message. The Kingdom of Heaven was at hand (Matthew 4:17). As Jesus called his disciples and began his healing ministry, He continued his message, proclaiming the gospel of the Kingdom (Matthew 4:23; 9:35; Luke 4:43; 8:1; 9:11). Jesus then gave his twelve disciples and later, the seventy, the assignment of announcing the arrival of the Kingdom of Heaven, confirming it with the healing of the sick, casting out demons, and raising the dead (Matthew 10:7, 8; Luke 10:8-11). In Acts, the Kingdom continued to be proclaimed. Paul persuaded the Jews of Ephesus regarding the Kingdom of God (Acts 19:8; 20:25). After arriving in Rome, Paul continued his mission to proclaim the Kingdom (Acts 28:23, 31). As Jesus had done, the disciples and Paul proclaimed the Kingdom. Now, so does every Christian as he declares the expansion of Jesus' Kingdom on earth through prayer and declaration.

As we continue to speak about something, the more our hearts turn toward the object of our words. Our declarations reveal what our most important values are and reflect back to Father what is the desire of His heart and will. Just as football fans continually talk about their favorite football team, declaring it to be great and continually hoping it will win the championship, the believer declares the reality of the ultimate victory of the Kingdom of God. However, different from rooting for a football team, the believer has real power in his prayer as he declares back to God his heart's desire that His Kingdom be expanded upon the earth.

Citizens of the kingdom

Right now, the nations of the earth have power over their assigned regions. Although it may not appear that way, the Bible declares that Jesus has all authority in Heaven and earth and therefore has authority even over the kings and rulers of the nations (Matthew 28:18-20; Romans 13:1-2). However, we know that one day, Jesus will return to physically rule his Kingdom upon the earth (1 Thessalonians 4:16-5:11).

For us, citizenship is not something that we think about all that often. We enjoy rights that sometimes we take for granted. However, those who do not enjoy rights of citizenship in any country, those we call refugees, are at a significant disadvantage. They do not have a country that they can call home. As followers of Jesus, we have a different type of citizenship, more valuable than any national citizenship. Citizenship in Heaven lifts the believer above the struggles of this world to hope in something greater and better (Philippians 3:20-21). This does not in any way mean that the believer ignores what is taking place on earth, but that he is not controlled by his circumstances. A believer disappointed in the outcome of an election does not need to despair because his candidate did not win. On the other hand, a believer whose candidate did win should not place his hope in the programs of his preferred candidate. In both situations he knows and affirms that Jesus has ultimate authority and all leaders will one day give an account to him for their leadership.

Of our four children, two were born in Italy and two in the United States. Scott and Sara are United States citizens because they were born here. However, Eric and Brian are also United States citizens even though they were not born in this country. They are citizens because Donelle and I are citizens of the United States. Furthermore, neither Eric nor Brian are Italian citizens even though they were born in that country. According to Italian law, they are not citizens because neither Donelle nor I are Italian citizens. After Eric, and later Brian, were born, we took each to the appropriate American authority in Italy. In Eric's case, it was the consulate in Florence. Brian, we took to the Embassy in Rome. With them, we brought their Italian birth certificates and our passports. On each occasion, we left with a State Department document declaring them to be United States citizens, their passport and their Social Security Card. Even though they had never been in the United States, they enjoyed all the rights, privileges and protections of a United States citizen. In Eric's case, he would be almost four before he ever set foot in this country; nevertheless during all that time he was a full United States citizen. Likewise, as children of our heavenly Father, even though we have never physically set foot in Heaven, we enjoy all the rights, privileges and protections of Heaven's citizenship.

In the Sermon on the Mount, Jesus spent considerable time teaching on the Kingdom of Heaven. He described who would be citizens of the Kingdom. In the first message, Jesus declared that the poor in spirit would receive the Kingdom of Heaven. In this statement, Jesus was not referring to those who are poor economically, but to those who recognize their spiritual poverty in relation to God. The poor in spirit have no means of making any claim upon God to save them. They have nothing to offer, but are in desperate and complete need of God to save them (Matthew 5:3).

As Jesus began the beatitudes with a definition of the Kingdom's citizens, he ended the teaching with the same. Those who would suffer persecution for Jesus' name would also receive the Kingdom of Heaven. The poor in spirit, having no other hope than Jesus, will live out of gratitude for him, rejecting all religious efforts to gain a positive standing with God. When we lived in Italy, many were shocked when we told them that we were sure about going to Heaven. They found the statement arrogant. They assumed that if you believe you are sure of going to Heaven then you must do certain things to make yourself "good enough" for God. If that were true, then believing that you will go to Heaven is arrogant. Religious people depend on following "rules" to make themselves "good enough" for Heaven. Lovers of Jesus receive Heaven as a gift, purchased for them by Jesus' death on the cross. However, throughout history, religious people maintaining their rules, persecute those who love Jesus and receive his gift of Heaven and salvation with grateful hearts.

Men, whether political or religious, desire recognition, but those who are wholly committed to Jesus cannot give it. That is why the early Christians refused to utter the statement "Caesar is Lord," preferring to perish in stead of denying the sole lordship of Jesus. Even Polycarp, the aged Bishop of Smyrna, refused to renounce Jesus and recognize Caesar as Lord though it would spare him from execution. He preferred to endure execution at the hands of the Romans than deny Jesus who had saved and sustained him throughout his long life. It is people like these, whom Jesus declared the Kingdom belonged (Matthew 5:10-11). The Kingdom of Heaven is not populated by those given to compromise. Because of what Jesus has done for them, they are ready and willing to sacrifice all for him. They know, like Peter did, that there is no one else to whom one may turn, since only Jesus has the words of eternal life (John 6:68). When you have found the treasure that will endure forever, what price is it to sacrifice that which you cannot hold on to? Due to their devotion to Jesus, citizens of the Kingdom will honor Jesus by keeping his commandments. The idea is not to be religious/legalistic, in hopes for a reward. As a loving wife seeks to please her husband only because she loves him and not because she hopes that he will provide a better life for her, so also citizens of the Kingdom follow Jesus, their spiritual husband (Ephesians 5:25-27). These Jesus-devoted individuals will be recognized as the greatest in the Kingdom of Heaven (Matthew 5:19). Their righteousness before God proves to be superior to that of religious/legalistic righteousness because it is founded on humility, gratitude and love, rather than effort and pride (Matthew 5:20). Jesus condemned Pharisaical righteousness because it came, not from heaven, but resulted from man's religious effort. In Matthew 6, Jesus contrasted the religious efforts of the Pharisees with true righteousness that Jesus looked for from his followers. True followers of Jesus live to please Father and nothing more. They do not seek recognition for their efforts as the Pharisees did. Citizens of the Kingdom gave to the poor, prayed, and fasted for the pleasure of Father, not for the audience of man.

Those who are citizens of the Kingdom will highly value the Kingdom of Heaven. Jesus tells us that they will seek it (Matthew 6:33; Luke 12:31). Only things of great value do we seek. In order to reveal this value of the Kingdom, Jesus told the parables of the Kingdom. Upon finding treasure in a field, a man sold everything he had in order to acquire the land (Matthew 13:44). A merchant, having discovered a valuable pearl, sold everything in order to purchase it (Matthew 13:45-46). These two parables describe what Jesus meant by seeking the Kingdom; obtaining the Kingdom is worth everything that we have, and all that we are. No amount of wealth, no possession and no amount of success can equal citizenship in the Kingdom of Heaven. The value of being a citizen of the Kingdom is one of the reasons we experience great joy when people meet Jesus. When the Philippian jailer came to Jesus, he and his entire household rejoiced greatly (Acts 16:34).

Jesus also warned that not everyone who thinks they are a citizen of the Kingdom will enter. Some will believe they are citizens of the Kingdom because of what they have done during their life-time. They've healed the sick and cast out demons, but Jesus will tell them that they are not citizens, because they did not have a relationship with him (Matthew 7:21-23). Even some known as "children of the Kingdom" will not enter the Kingdom of Heaven, but some who appeared to be far from the Kingdom will be welcomed inside (Matthew 8:11-12; Luke 13:28-29). It is only those who have received a new identity from Jesus who will be the citizens of the Kingdom (John 3:3-5). The real value of citizenship in the Kingdom is knowing Jesus. Without Jesus, the Kingdom of Heaven loses all value. Therefore, it is the character of Jesus that defines the citizen of the Kingdom. They are not great as the world defines great, because Jesus was not considered great by the world. Jesus defined greatness in terms of a child. As a child is humble, so are citizens of the Kingdom (Matthew 11:28-30; 18:1-4). According to Jesus, children symbolize the Kingdom of Heaven (Matthew 19:14: Mark 10:14-15; Luke 18:16-17). Not only are children the symbol of the Kingdom, but those considered great in the world are actually at risk of not becoming citizens of the Kingdom at all (Matthew 19:23-24; Mark 10:24-25; Luke 18:24-25). Jesus went so far as to say that from the world's perspective, it is impossible for the "successful" to enter, but with God it is still possible.

As Jesus demonstrated, there exist hindrances to becoming a citizen of the Kingdom, but there are even those who seek to hinder others from entering the Kingdom. False teachers travel throughout the world deceiving others and blinding them from the light (Matthew 23:13-15). However, in the end it will be Jesus who will invite his own to enter the Kingdom of Heaven as citizens (Matthew 25:34).

Kingdom described

If we are going to be citizens of the Kingdom, it is important for us to know what it is. Early in American history, foreigners came to study the United States of America to determine what made it tick. Some like Alexis de Tocqueville wrote their findings down and published their description of the United States. The New Testament also gives us a glimpse of the Kingdom of Heaven. Modern countries are the glory and power of men, particularly those who are ruling at any given time. Former presidents write their memoirs to give a written record of the glory of their administration. However, the Kingdom of Heaven reflects Jesus' glory and power (Matthew 6:13). The New Testament reveals that the Kingdom of Heaven is more powerful than the kingdoms of this world (Matthew 12:28). As time goes by, it will not diminish, but rather permeate the entire world (Matthew 13:13). In his instruction to Peter and the other disciples, Jesus implied that the Kingdom of Heaven on earth would be a reflection of the Kingdom in Heaven (Matthew 16:19). Because of the Kingdom's value, glory and power, Jesus called men to leave everything in order to call others to enter into the Kingdom (Luke 9:60-62). Jesus' Kingdom is not what men would expect. As Jesus told Pilate, Jesus' Kingdom is not of this world (John 18:36). It's nature resides in Heaven but is being brought to earth through the church. Jesus' Kingdom is not natural to the earth; it must come from Heaven.

Because of the power associated with the Kingdom of Heaven, citizens of the Kingdom are freed from fear and anxiety. Although citizens of the Kingdom may experience anxiety and worry, they do so unnecessarily, because Jesus called his followers never to allow anxiety to reside in their life. Citizens of the Kingdom may experience these feelings because they believe the lies of this world and ignore the promises of the Kingdom (Matthew 6:25-34). When Jesus endured the anxiety of the Garden of Gethsemane and defeated the horrors of death on the cross, there was nothing left to cause us anxiety (Luke 12:32).

Finally, the disciples understood and Jesus confirmed that the Kingdom of Heaven would continue to have a special relationship with the nation of Israel (Acts 1:6; Romans 11:25-31). Before Jesus' ascension, the disciples asked if Jesus was restoring the Kingdom to Israel. Jesus did not correct their assumption, but he did tell them it was not time. To the Romans, Paul explained that Israel had gone through a temporary hardening so that the nations could enter into the Kingdom; then

Declaring God's Kingdom

Israel itself would enter. The follower of Jesus may possess citizenship in a nation currently on earth, but this is temporary. The follower's true identity is in Heaven as a citizen of the Kingdom. Since our identity defines how we will live, no Christian should allow his temporary national citizenship to negatively impact his permanent Heavenly Kingdom citizenship.

Summary

In Heaven and on earth, Jesus is the legitimate and legal ruler. As his followers declare in prayer and proclaim through evangelism and teaching, the Kingdom of Heaven is expanded on earth. Jesus' Kingdom is not like that of men. It does not depend on worldly power or force, but expands through prayer, humility and declaration. Jesus' Kingdom is not discouraged by apparent set-backs on earth or when immoral men gain power. Jesus' Kingdom does not place hope in apparent victories when godly men win elections or despair when ungodly men rule. The citizen of the Kingdom looks beyond the rule of man to declare good upon the earth.

The fact that we are children of God impacts our relationship to the Kingdom. Paul declared to the Philippians that we are citizens, but the Kingdom is also our Father's which means it is ours to inherit. The Kingdom we declare through prayer is ours. When I was in college, I worked for Sears and attempted to be the best employee I could. Nevertheless, my name was not "Sears." If it had been, I believe my perspective would have been quite different, because I would have been working in the family business. For followers of Jesus, the kingdom is our family business!

Declaring God's Kingdom

Questions for Reflection

1. How does your citizenship in Heaven impact how you view your earthly citizenship?

2. How might the fact that we are at war with spiritual forces help us understand and endure the difficulties we face as Christians?

3. What benefits of Kingdom citizenship do we enjoy now while living upon the earth?

4. How does the reality that the Kingdom is our family business change your understanding of it?

Papa, I acknowledge my purpose on earth is not for me, but to see your Kingdom extended on earth. I acknowledge that my existence is to promote your Kingdom. I declare your Kingdom upon the earth to see it transform the lives of men and women for you glory, removing them from the slavery of being conformed to this world. Amen.

Chapter 5
Expanding God's Will On Earth As In Heaven
Matthew 6:10

Anyone who has participated in team sports knows the importance of each player listening and implementing what the coach taught. For even one player to ignore the coach's instructions and do what he wants can be disaster for the team. For all the players to follow their own will instead of applying the coordinated instructions of the coach results in chaos. It is curious how often the team filled with the most talented players does not win the championship. Rather, it is the team that applies the program of the coach and plays together that wins. Following the will of God in place of our own will has much in common with a team working together with their coach to achieve goals that they could not reach if they followed their own will independently from their coach.

When we voluntarily place ourselves under someone's authority, there are potential risks. When we make that decision, we place our control and desires under their authority. That being the case, we need to make sure we completely trust the individual under whose care we are ready to live. When we pray for Father's will to be done on earth as it is in heaven, we declare that we are ready and willing to submit our own will and desires to those of Father, even when we may not agree with Father's will.

This third command adds a new aspect not found in the previous two. Following the command for God's will to occur, a comparison is offered to describe in what manner it is to come. God's will is desired, but it is declared back to Father that as His will is manifested in Heaven, it also be done on earth. In making this command/declaration, the believer desires that what takes place in Heaven where Father's will is perfectly implemented, takes place on earth now. This declaration does not merely ask that Father's will be done on earth at sometime in the future, like during the millennium, but is a declaration that it take place immediately.

Praying that Father's will become reality on earth as it is in Heaven means that we understand how Father's will is made reality in Heaven. Typically a person assumes that Father's will is the same as his own. This assumption is made without adequately considering that the person's will and Father's will may be conflicting. A conflict between Father's will and an individual's will would require the person to submit his own will to Father's. Jesus did exactly this while praying in the Garden of Gethsemane. Jesus' prayer in the Garden revealed that Father had a better way than what Jesus' will desired (Matthew 26:39). To fulfill Father's will carried a price tag for Jesus. In the same way, in order to see Father's will manifested upon the earth, it may require both change and submission on our part, because we may have to endure some things that we do not wish to go through.

God's Will: What it is?

When we consider the topic of declaring that God's will be revealed and fulfilled on earth as it is in heaven, we should also take some time to consider what God's will is. To do so, we should consider the question of what God the Father desires to take place or what He does not want to take place. For example, Jesus declared that it is outside the will of God for any children to perish (Matthew 18:14). Peter declared a similar sentiment when he wrote that Father desires for all men to come to a point of repentance (2 Peter 3:9).

Jesus himself prayed the same prayer that he commanded his disciples to pray. He commanded that the Father's will be done, even though the Father's will differed from what he

Expanding God's Kingdom On Earth As In Heaven

desired. In Jesus' case, the fulfillment of the Father's will meant his own suffering (Matthew 26:42; Luke 22:42). In Luke, Jesus' prayer is represented by a command; "Father, if You are willing, remove this cup from Me; yet not My will, but Yours be done." The passage in Luke is curious, because prior to Jesus' prayer/command about Father's will, he issued a conditional statement that he assumed to be true – "if/since you are willing, remove this cup from Me." The conditional Greek form used here assumes the truth of the statement. Unfortunately, this meaning is lost in the English translation. Jesus assumed that Father was willing; then he issued a command to remove the cup. Following that, he prayed/commanded/declared Father's will to be done. In his latter declaration, Jesus used a different word from the word, "will," used earlier. We could translate the first part of Jesus' statement as "since you are willing, remove this cup from me." Followed by "but your determined purpose/will be done." This prayer reveals the internal conflict that was in Father and Son. Jesus recognized that Father's heart was that the cup be removed, but that His intended purpose must prevail; therefore he must go to the cross.

At times, we must distinguish between Father's determined purpose and His heart's desire. In the case of Jesus, Father's intended purpose was that Jesus die for the sake of man (Isaiah 53:10), but Jesus' prayer in the Garden indicates that Father's heart desire was different. The same might be said of the earlier verses indicating Father's desire that all men come to repentance. We might say that it is Father's heart desire that all men come to repentance, but His intended purpose won't overrule man's responsibility for his own decisions. Father will not overrule man's personal responsibility for his decisions, even though it would be what Father's heart desires and what would benefit the individual. Love of man and respect for man's individual responsibility requires that man be responsible for his choice, either to repent and turn to God, or to maintain his self-destructive course inherited from Adam.

Parents experience a similar dilemma with their children. No parent enjoys disciplining his/her children. Many, if not all, would prefer not to, because it is hard for all involved. Nevertheless, the wise parent provides the correction for the higher good of instructing the child he/she loves. In fact, it is commonly understood that a parent who fails to discipline his/her child does not reflect love for the child. Father is the perfect parent who disciplines out of love, but who also refuses to force or manipulate His children to do what he wants.

God's will toward Jesus' followers

Jesus also revealed Father's intention for those who turn to Jesus. Father gave to Jesus a certain assurance that all that had been given to him would be brought securely to the day of resurrection (John 6:39; 1 John 2:17). Jesus' words quoted in John remind us of the promise that Paul gave to the Philippians, that God is able to complete the good work of salvation that he began in us (Philippians 1:6). Through Jesus' work of redemption, it was Father's will that the believer be sanctified (Hebrews 10:10). In stating that he would lose none of those whom Father had given to him, Jesus meant that all those individuals would receive eternal life, because it was Father's will/purpose to resurrect them on the last day. However, the ultimate purpose of God's will is not man-directed but God-directed. All exists in order to give glory to God according to His will (Revelation 4:11).

In his letter to the Romans, Paul implied that at times, the will of God may be contingent on other events; therefore he asked the believers to pray. Paul urged the Roman believers to pray along with him that he would be rescued from his Jewish enemies. Contrary to what we might think, the intended purpose of their prayers was not merely for Paul to be free, but that the will of God for Paul to go to Rome, would be fulfilled (Romans

Expanding God's Kingdom On Earth As In Heaven

15:30-31). In this case, the Jewish opposition seemed to be hindering the fulfillment of the will of God; therefore, the believers were called to intercede with prayer to overcome the opposition. Paul's request sheds additional light on the connection and importance of our prayer with the fulfillment of the will of God. Paul's call to the Roman believers to pray was not merely a spiritual exercise, but an act of faith, because believers are assured of God's response as they pray according to His will (1 John 5:14).

At other times, Paul referred to the will of God as an affirmation of truth fulfilled. Numerous times, Paul introduced himself to a local congregation as an apostle of Jesus through the means of the will of God (1 Corinthians 1:1, 2 Corinthians 2:1; Ephesians 1:1; Colossians 1:1; 2 Timothy 1:1). The believers in Macedonia insisted on being a part of those churches contributing to the relief effort in Palestine according to the will of God (2 Corinthians 8:5). Through God's will that Jesus gave himself for our sins, we believers today are also delivered from the evil that exists in the current age (Galatians 1:4).

God's will for us goes beyond forgiveness and eternal life, but also includes being adopted into God's family (Ephesians 1:5). In Ephesians 1:11, we read a description of the intentions of God. God intended to predestine men for an eternal inheritance. His choice is accomplished according to the "counsel" of his "will." In this verse, Paul indicated that God's purposes were connected to His will. We might say that God's purposes receive counsel from God's will. The picture formed for us is that God's purposes are not random, but are well thought out in order to achieve their intended results.

In other places, Paul revealed some of the content of God's will. To the Colossians, Paul revealed that he continually prayed for them to be filled with the acknowledgment of God's will. Paul wanted the Colossians to not only possess an intellectual

77

knowledge of God's will, but to be able to recognize it when it occurred in their lives. Their acknowledgment of God's will implied that they would experience it in some manner. A little later, Paul related to the Colossians the desire that they possess a complete and full knowledge of the will of God (Colossians 4:12).

Paul's discussion of the will of God with the Colossians implies that the believer is to have a deep and extensive grasp of God's will. The believer's knowledge of God's will is not to be theoretical, but both intellectual and experiential. The will of God also has a moral component. God's intent for all believers is that they avoid sexual immorality (1 Thessalonians 4:3). Through moral living, believers silence those who oppose Jesus and accomplish the will of God (1 Peter 4:2). It is also God's desire that believers practice joy, prayer and thanksgiving (1 Thessalonians 5:16-18).

As Jesus discovered, the purposes of God for him would result in suffering. Peter revealed to his readers that they could experience the same thing. Believers are called to do what is right, which may also result in suffering. God's purposes do not include the believer's decision to avoid suffering by doing what is wrong (1 Peter 3:17). If it is the will of God that the believer's obedience lead to man's persecution for the sake of Jesus, then the believer, like Jesus, entrusts his/her soul to Father (1 Peter 4:19). Furthermore, what drives the believer is the will of God (1 Peter 4:2). Peter's discussion of God's will, contrasting with living according to the flesh, reminds us of the contrast that Paul made in Romans 8 between walking by the flesh and by the Spirit. In this way, there could be a connection drawn between walking with the Spirit and living according to the will of God.

Expanding God's Kingdom On Earth As In Heaven

Our responsibility

Our relationship to God's will is not to be passive, but we are instructed to declare Father's will to be done on earth. However, Jesus' instruction is actually stronger than simply asking that it happen. Jesus gave the request as a command. We are to command that Father's will be done on earth (Matthew 6:10). Further, in the Sermon on the Mount, Jesus indicated an additional responsibility that we have regarding the will of God. We are to do it! (Matthew 7:21) Paul indicated that it was possible to know the will of God, but not do it (Romans 2:17-18). The Jews knew the will of God through the revelation of the Old Testament Scriptures, but in rejecting Jesus, they did not do the will of God and placed themselves under His condemnation.

As the Jews knew the will of God, Jesus' command to do the will of God implies that we already know it. We've already seen the content of God's will as it is revealed to us through the Bible. One of the responsibilities that Jesus gave to his disciples, beginning with the original twelve and continuing to every generation of disciples until Jesus returns, is for them to teach peoples of all nations what Jesus commanded us to do (Matthew 28:18-20; 2 Timothy 2:2). As one generation of disciples instructs others on what Jesus commanded, the content of Father's will would also be included either explicitly or implicitly. For example, Jesus commanded his disciples to proclaim the kingdom of God. Implied in his command is Father's will that all people come to repentance, which is explicitly stated in Scripture. However, Jesus also commanded his disciples to heal the sick, cast out demons, cleanse the lepers and raise the dead. Jesus' additional commands in the same context (Matthew 10:7-8) imply that it is Father's will that Satan's kingdom of disease and death be destroyed by Jesus' followers. In the Old Testament, David wrote that the Messiah would forgive all our iniquities and heal all of our diseases. If it is the Father's will that Jesus take on all of our sins/iniquities, then the implication is that it is also Father's will that he heals us of all our diseases (Psalm 103:3).

Part of God's will, we have already come to know, is the mystery of our redemption in Jesus, which was clearly declared in the Old Testament, but not understood by the Jews until Jesus came, died and rose again (Ephesians 1:9). Although we know, understand, and experience the redemptive part of God's will, we are commanded to also comprehend/understand what the will of God is (Ephesians 5:17). Paul's command here goes beyond an intellectual and experiential knowledge, but indicates that we are to understand the implications of God's will. The word used here indicates a putting together, like the child's game of connect the dots, to reveal the complete picture. Until we go through the exercise of connecting the dots, we have not come to full understanding. The following verses imply a moral response to God's will; "do not be drunk with wine", but also a spiritual component, which is "be filled with the Holy Spirit." There is also a worship component as follows; speaking to one another with Psalms and in spiritual songs, as well as giving thanks (Ephesians 5:19-20).

There is a part of God's will that is clearly revealed to us, but Paul's language indicates that there is another part which we are to understand without it being explicitly stated. Jesus seemed to expect this from his disciples and marveled when they didn't grasp it. After they told him to send the people away to get food, Jesus told his disciples to give them something to eat (Matthew 14:16). When they balked at the command, Jesus showed them how. Based on Jesus' warning about the leaven of the Pharisees and Herod, the disciples assumed that Jesus was talking about the bread they had forgotten to take with them. Jesus expected them to understand that they didn't need to worry about bread anymore, since he had shown them how to feed the five thousand and then again the four thousand. He expected them to understand that he was warning them about the teaching of the Pharisees and Herod (Mark 8:14-21).

It is as if God supplies the "if" part of the statement and we are responsible to arrive at the "then" part. If, with Jesus, the disciples can feed the five thousand, then they no longer need to worry about bread or any material need any more. While Jesus didn't explicitly say the latter, he clearly expected them to live by it. On the other hand, Jesus reserved his greatest praise for the centurion who requested Jesus not to enter his home in order to heal his servant, because he understood Jesus' authority. Jesus didn't need to be present; all he needed to do was say the word. The centurion understood that he as an officer had the authority to issue a command to a soldier and it would be done, even though he didn't actually observe the obedience. Jesus being an even greater man, with even more authority, surely would have a similar power over disease. Jesus praised this man and even marveled at his faith, declaring that he had never observed such a faith in all of Israel (Matthew 8:5-13). The centurion grasped without being taught that if Jesus was who he revealed himself to be, then it would not be necessary for him to be present in order to heal the servant. The centurion became a model of how we are to live out the will of God.

This concept of comprehending the will of God opens up a whole new area of living out God's will. Not only are we responsible to follow what Jesus' taught directly, but under the guidance of the Holy Spirit, we are to exercise our faith and live out the implications of all that he taught, which isn't specifically stated. This may be what the author of Hebrews refers to in Hebrews 6:1-2, when he urged his readers to go beyond what we often assume is the bulk of Christianity: repentance, faith, instruction about cleansing and laying on of hands (which refers to receiving gifts, healing and appointing leaders), eternal life and the coming judgment. In his statement, the author of Hebrews exhorts his readers to expand their walk with Jesus beyond where most Christians live their life. When we live out by faith the implications of Jesus' teaching and expect him to do more than what he explicitly said in the Bible, we cause Jesus to marvel at our faith.

Finally, we are responsible to develop an affection for the will of God. We are not to follow the will of God out of mere obligation, although that is better than not following it at all; but we are to do the will of the Father from our heart (Ephesians 6:6). We live by the will of God from our heart, because our first desire is to please God rather than seeking the praise of men.

Who does God's will?

Those who practice the will of the Father are identified as being in an intimate familial relationship with Jesus. When Jesus' mother and brothers came to see him, Jesus declared that it is only those who do the will of God who are his mother, brothers and sisters. By so saying, Jesus revealed that kingdom relationships have a stronger tie than physical and natural relationships (Matthew 12:50; Mark 3:35). Natural relationships are temporary and limited to this world, but kingdom relationships are eternal. Husbands and wives will no longer be married couples after the resurrection. Neither will our children remain our children in the resurrection, although family members may all be brothers and sisters in Christ.

To Nicodemus, Jesus revealed that this relationship occurs through a supernatural work of the Holy Spirit who bestows life in an individual, which Jesus explained to the curious Pharisee as being born again (John 3:5-8). Earlier in his Gospel, John had indicated that the event of being "born again" is the result of the Father's will (John 1:13). To assist us in understanding what it means to do the will of God, Scripture gives us examples. God himself identified King David as one man who was a man after God's own heart and did all of God's will (Acts 13:22). To Ananias, Paul was revealed as another who would know the will of God (Acts 22:14).

Benefits of doing God's will

Jesus never tells us to do anything that is not good for us. We may not understand why Jesus tells us to do something or what the benefits are. However, we do know that because of his love for us, his instructions are good. Therefore, we should expect that there are benefits from doing Father's will and praying/declaring/commanding that His will be done on earth as it is in heaven.

The world teaches that everything is defined by the physical. Modern psychology teaches that we must have our physical needs met first before we can be happy. Jesus taught that the Kingdom of God does not operate on that paradigm. He taught that there are needs more important than our physical needs. This does not mean that our physical needs are unimportant to Jesus, just that there are needs more important to our survival and happiness. Jesus illustrated this after speaking to the Samaritan woman. The disciples had gone into the village to get food while he remained at the well. At the well, he introduced the Kingdom of God to the Samaritan woman, who then went into town to tell all those she knew. In the meantime, the disciples urged Jesus to eat some food, but Jesus responded that his food comes from doing the will of the Father (John 4:34). Jesus' words imply that our physical well-being is more tied to our doing the will of the Father than eating. For most of us, that is a surprising concept. But it helps us understand how people from the most affluent nation in the world can be so miserable.

83

Expanding God's Kingdom On Earth As In Heaven

While Jesus pointed out a physical benefit from doing the will of the Father, there are also spiritual benefits. For the Jews, Jesus was hard to comprehend. One of the things that caused them to marvel was the fact that he had such a vast knowledge of Scripture and the Jewish Law, but had never been formally educated. Jesus explained how this was possible. What Jesus taught was not his own; he received it from the Father. Jesus claimed to be merely the spokesman (John 7: 16). This was a very humble statement coming from Jesus, the one through whom the whole creation came into being (John 1:3). Jesus pointed out to the Jews, that those who did Father's will would recognize that Jesus' teaching was from Father and not something that he made up (John 7:17). Jesus' point was that as we practice the will of Father, we will grow in our knowledge of the truth. Not only do those who practice Father's will recognize truth, but they do so because in so doing, their minds are renewed (Romans 12:2). Practicing God's will has the powerful impact of changing the way that we think.

From an unexpected source, we grasp a third benefit to doing God's will. The man who was born blind had an amazing grasp of who the Messiah would be. When the Jews claimed ignorance to where Jesus came from, the blind man posed to them a question to which they could not respond. Jesus was doing things that only someone from God could do (John 9:27-31). Earlier, one of their own, Nicodemus, had noted the same thing (John 3:1-2). Here, a man born blind who had received no formal education in the law informed them of what they already knew but refused to admit. Those who fear God and practice His will have God's ear (John 9:31). The man born blind grasped the relational benefit of those who do Father's will; God listens to their prayers and requests.

The author of the letter to the Hebrews pointed out a future benefit of doing the will of Father. After we live our life practicing Father's will, we will receive our reward (Hebrews

10:36). In order for us to reach that future point, God gives us all what we need so that we can do His will right now (Hebrews 13:21). Jesus told his disciples that he would not leave them as orphans, but that he would come to them and remain with them right up to the end of the present age when he will return (John 14:18; Matthew 28:20).

Jesus and God's will

Not only does Jesus give us benefits for living according to the will of Father, but he lived it out himself. Father's will was what motivated Jesus. Again, Jesus modeled a different way of living than we find normal on earth. Normally, people live in ways so that their own needs and desires are met first. Some people make this more of a focus than others, but we are all naturally self-serving to some degree. Jesus modeled a different, kingdom approach to living. He not only did Father's will; he desired to do Father's will (John 5:30). We tend to put doing Father's will in the area of duty or obligation, because we don't view it as enjoyable. However, Jesus desired to do the will of Father; it was his delight to do so and gave him pleasure to live in that manner. Doing Father's will was both his desire and purpose in life. Jesus left heaven to become a man on earth for the purpose of accomplishing, not his desires, but Father's will (John 6:38; Hebrews 10:7, 9; Psalm 40:7-8). Actually, all men have been created to do the will of Father, but we have abdicated our original purpose, thinking we found a superior way to live; Jesus, on the other hand faithfully lived out his purpose. Praying/declaring that God's will be done on earth is not merely a future event, but a present purpose for every believer. We are to live like Jesus who lived out Father's will for him and found joy in so doing. As we follow his example, we will receive the same benefits that Jesus did.

Expanding God's Kingdom On Earth As In Heaven

Summary

Before we begin praying for God's will to be done on earth, we should consider what the implications are. First, we are declaring ourselves in submission to Father's will. Second, we declare that we desire Father's will even when it may conflict with our own. Third, our declaration means that we are fully willing to endure the consequences as well as the blessings that come from God's will being fulfilled on earth as it is in heaven. Like Jesus, we are to make the fulfillment of Father's will in our life and in the world the purpose of our life. To live according to the prayer, Jesus indicated to live a radically different life than the normal human life. While the majority of men live governed by their own will and desires, Jesus' prayer leads to a life of submission to Father's perfect heart and will.

Questions for Reflection

1. Reflect on a time when it became apparent to you that the Father's will was different from what you desired. How did you respond?

2. What does it mean to you to live out the implications of eternal life?

3. In what ways do you discover the will of God for your life?

Papa, too often I believe that Your will is merely an extension of what I want. I recognize that this was not the case with Jesus. In this world, it was Your will that Jesus faced tribulation from men to accomplish your purposes. Father, I submit my will and desires to Yours, because I recognize that Your plan and purposes are greater than my limited view, perspective and desires. May Your reign and will be extended in my life and throughout the earth. As it is, help me to live out my purpose in your kingdom. Amen.

Chapter 6
Declaring to God Our Needs
Matthew 6:11

When I was about ten years old, my dad wanted to teach me about the value of money and making a purchase. So he told me to pick out anything in the store that cost a dollar or less and he would purchase it for me. Obviously a dollar purchased much more then than it does today. He took me to a discount store for me to make my selection. In a limited, way my dad placed himself under my authority. He would purchase whatever I told him I wanted. I still remember what I purchased. It was a kit motor that my dad and I later built together. In the Lord's prayer, Jesus revealed to his followers a relationship similar to that experience with my dad so many years ago.

The fourth command, found in verse 11, reveals a shift. The previous three commands were issued in relationship to things. Those were God's name, God's kingdom, and God's will. However in this fourth command, the command is issued directly to God. Jesus instructed his disciples to issue a command to Father for Him to give to them their daily bread. It is this command that takes outrageous prayer to the next level. How can we, God's creation and children, issue to Him direct commands? Should not Jesus have softened these requests in some manner? Why didn't he phrase them as questions? "Would you give us our daily bread?"

The direct nature of this command indicates a profound intimacy between God and His child. This is the way a child might speak to his parents or with whom he is extremely familiar. We express our needs in such a direct way with only those that we know intimately. It is not the way that we would speak with a stranger.

Intimacy

In this command, Jesus reveals that it is within our authority to go before God and issue Him a command as our Helper to provide for us what we need for that day. On multiple occasions, the Old Testament revealed God as man's Helper (Psalm 33:20; 70:5; 115:9). Hesitancy to seek the help of God in a direct manner may not reveal so much humility, but a certain distance from God. Children do not put on airs to get what they need from a parent whom they know loves them. They get to the point and can be pointed, even appearing rude in their action. Not that we are to be rude with God, but Jesus' words imply that we can be bold and direct in bringing our needs to the attention of Father. In Matthew 6:33, Jesus promised to those who were dedicated to the Kingdom of God, that Father would provide for all their physical needs. Based on this promise, a believer has the authority to address God boldly.

God as our helper is often reflected in every family. Think about who serves whom in a family. Are the preschoolers fixing dinner, going to work, and paying the mortgage? Of course not, they enjoy the benefits of their parents' love, care and service. Parents lovingly respond to their children's demands because they love them. In the same way, Father has humbled Himself to provide for our needs and demands, because He loves us and delights in providing for us.

Jesus' direction to his disciples in the Lord's Prayer to address God as "Father" reinforces the concept of intimacy with God. In the Old Testament, a few were considered to be friends of God and as such, took bold approaches to Him. Abraham boldly addressed God in relation to the intended destruction of Sodom. Knowing God as well as he did, Abraham made some assumptions on what God would and would not do. Since God had revealed Himself to be righteous, Abraham knew that God would never destroy Sodom if fifty righteous men were dwelling there (Genesis 18:23-24). He repeated his assumption if forty-five righteous were dwelling there (Genesis 18:28). Finally, he recognized that he may be stretching the bounds of their relationship when he asked God not to be angry, but assumed that God would not even destroy Sodom if only ten righteous men dwelt there (Genesis 18:32). Abraham's bold approach with God revealed a certain intimacy with God. God had revealed to Abraham His righteous nature, so that Abraham could make bold assumptions and declarations to God. These declarations were met, not with anger or frustration, but with acceptance from God.

Centuries after Abraham, Moses repeated Abraham's bold approach. In response to Israel's flagrant sin in constructing and worshiping the golden calves, God declared that He would destroy all of Israel and make Moses into a great nation. By so doing, God would still fulfill his promise to make Abraham into a great nation, because Moses was a physical descendant of Abraham through Isaac, Jacob and Levi. In order to preempt any attempt by Moses to protect Israel, God commanded Moses to be quiet (Exodus 32:10). However, Moses made a bold move. He ignored God's injunction to him and plead for the salvation of Israel (Genesis 32:11). In so doing, Moses, like Abraham had, revealed an intimate relationship with God. Scripture's surprising statement that God changed His mind about Israel, indicates the closeness of Moses' relationship with Him (Genesis 32:14). Neither Abraham nor Moses dared refer to God as Father, yet Jesus commanded his disciples to approach God in that bold manner. John understood the concept when he declared that all who receive Jesus are given the right to become children of God (John 1:12). The Lord's Prayer is one of the ways in which the Father-child relationship between God and believer is applied. If Abraham and Moses could boldly approach God, even though the Father-child relationship had not yet been revealed, how much more can the believer in Jesus boldly address God to do what He has promised.

Bread

In the fourth command, Jesus instructed his disciples to approach God with a command/declaration for their daily bread. Of all the things that Jesus could have directed them to seek from God, it was bread. Therefore, it is important to note the central role that bread takes in the New Testament. Bread in the New Testament, as it does in our day refers to that which is necessary for for physical life. In the Bible, the mention of bread often referred to literal bread, but today it can also refer to money, needed to purchase the things of life. When Jesus instructed his followers to come to God for their daily bread, they make a broadly based request/command.

It is interesting that the first reference to bread in the New Testament is in the context of temptation to sin. It was the first temptation Satan issued to Jesus, tempting him to use his powers independently from the direction of the Holy Spirit, to meet his own needs. This is a similar temptation that he used to trip up Eve. It was within Jesus' power to meet his needs, but it was not what the Holy Spirit had directed him. In the Garden, it was within Eve's power to reach out and take the fruit from the tree of the knowledge of good and evil, despite God's command not to eat from that tree (Genesis 3:1-3; Matthew 4:3; Luke 4:3).

Where Adam and Eve failed, Jesus triumphed. In response to Satan's temptation, Jesus gave a kingdom truth; man does not live by bread (physical bread) alone, but by every word from Father. Our life depends, not on physical sustenance, but on Father's sustaining life and power (Matthew 4:4; Luke 4:4). Jesus' response clearly reveals that we have greater needs than physical. Perhaps this is why this command comes fourth in the Lord's Prayer; other more important issues are addressed, such as God's holiness, His Kingdom, and His will.

The kindness of God to supply our bread

Ever since Adam and Eve chose to follow Satan's lead and ignore God's instruction, man has consistently questioned the goodness of God. At the core of Satan's temptation was his implication that God was not good. First he implied that God had prohibited the fruit of all the trees from them (Genesis 3:1). When Eve quoted God's instruction, Satan boldly declared that God was lying. "You will not die," he affirmed, contradicting the warning God had given to them (Genesis 3:4). He sealed the deal when he implied that God was holding back from them and that they would become like God but God didn't want that (Genesis 3:5). After Satan's lying assault, all Eve had to do was see that the fruit on the tree of the knowledge of good and evil was appealing to her eye, and her failure was complete. Adam quickly followed suit. From that day forward, men have consistently jumped to the conclusion that God is hesitant to help them.

Consider the question the leper posed to Jesus. You could heal me if you were willing (Mark 1:40). Without saying it, the leper knew that Jesus had the power to heal, but he doubted whether he would. This assumption is common today among Christians who say or believe that God could help them, but are just not sure whether He will. We claim that this is faith, but it is actually questioning the goodness of God's character and implying that our heavenly Father is less kind than we are, because we would help someone if we could.

In the Sermon on the Mount, Jesus countered this type of mistaken thinking about our Father. Jesus described the normal kindly response of any human father. If his child asked for bread, he would never think of tricking his dear child by offering him a stone that might appear as a loaf of bread. That would be cruel. No loving father would do that. Jesus repeated and reinforced his lesson by repeating the concept with a child asking

93

for a fish and the father giving a serpent. It is common knowledge that no good father would take such an action (Matthew 7:9; Luke 11:11). Then Jesus drew the all-important conclusion. If human fathers, who are evil, would not do anything so cruel, then our heavenly Father, who perfectly loves, will give to us what we need (Matthew 7:11). Jesus' affirmation of the Father's goodness confirms what he had earlier taught about avoiding worry. God's children are not to worry about what they will eat or what they will wear, because their heavenly Father feeds even the sparrows and clothes the wild flowers in splendor. If He does that for them, He will surely do more for His own children (Matthew 6:25-30). All we have to do is ask and wait.

With the disciples, Jesus took the lesson a step farther. In Sunday School, children learn that Jesus fed the five thousand and again the four thousand. However something more than Jesus feeding the multitudes took place. We have already seen that the disciples fed the multitudes through Jesus' power. On the occasion of feeding the five thousand when Jesus' disciples urged him to take action and provide for the crowds, Jesus turned to them and told them to feed the people. On each occasion, their response implied that they couldn't, but Jesus showed them how they could. Each time, he took whatever they had, blessed it, and then told them to give it to everyone there (Matthew 14:15-21). On the occasion of the four thousand, it was Jesus who had compassion for the people. When the disciples doubted whether anything of substance could be done because of their meager supplies, Jesus showed them what to do (Matthew 15:32-38). On both occasions, the disciples ended up with more bread than they began with.

The feeding of the multitudes is a principle of Kingdom economics. Ordinary math doesn't work. While we can't explain it, little becomes more than enough. Over the years, many Christians seeking to honor God give a tenth of their income

Declaring To God Our Needs

without understanding how they will pay all their bills, but somehow, each day their needs are met and each month, all their bills are paid. They can't explain it according to math and budgets, but their heavenly Father takes care of them. This is what Jesus meant when he said to declare that Father provide for our daily bread.

In Luke, Jesus gave another important kingdom principle about asking, and that is persistence. This principle does not mean that we have to convince God, but that at times, we need to ask persistently. Jesus told the story of a neighbor who knocked on the door at midnight to get a loaf of bread. Although the owner might be slow and resistant to giving the bread, he will do so if the man persists in knocking and asking. Jesus taught his disciples that we also are to ask and keep asking, because God will respond and we will receive (Luke 11:5-10). On another occasion, Jesus taught his disciples to pray and keep praying until they receive their answer. This was the point of the widow's request before the unjust judge. Jesus is clear that our Father is not like the judge, but a contrast of the judge (Luke 18:7-8). Although persistence may be required in the asking, seeking and knocking, when God responds he will act quickly.

Upon reading Jesus' teaching in Luke, we question why God doesn't respond immediately. In the example cited above about the persistent widow (Luke 18:1-8), Jesus told the parable to teach his disciples persistence in prayer. Jesus wants his followers to persistently pursue that which is needed, while at the same time never doubting the goodness and generosity of their heavenly Father. When it is time, Father will respond quickly to his children. An incident from Daniel's life reveals another component that we who live with the constraints of the material world may not immediately grasp. In an effort to further understand the great revelations God had given to him, Daniel prayed and fasted for further understanding (Daniel 10:2-3). For three weeks, Daniel persisted in asking for this revelation. Finally an angel appeared to him with an explanation. Daniel's request had been granted immediately, but the angel had been delayed due to someone he referred to as the prince of Persia (Daniel 10:13). Not until another angel, Michael, who in Jude is identified as an arch (chief) angel came to his assistance, could the angel reach Daniel (Daniel 10:13; Jude 1:9).

The persistence exemplified in Daniel and taught in the parable of the widow in Luke 18, reveals that there is resistance to the plans of God which believers need to overcome through prayer. Daniel's experience indicates that, while God is not slow to answer, a favorable response may be delayed due to opposition.

Spiritual/worship references to bread

While the request for our heavenly Father to supply our daily bread is clearly a reference to physical bread, the concept is also used in the New Testament to teach spiritual truths. After the episodes of feeding the five thousand and the four thousand, the disciples forgot to take bread with them for their journey across the Sea of Galilee. Their lack of material provision clearly concerned the disciples. When Jesus told them to watch out for the leaven of the Pharisees, they thought he was upset because they forgot to bring bread to eat. Jesus revealed to them how absurd their conclusion was since they had just fed the five thousand with less than they had for the four thousand, yet ended up with more than with which they began. His point was to not worry at all about having physical food, because it would be provided. It was only then that they grasped that when Jesus referred to the leaven of the Pharisees he meant to watch out for their teaching (Matthew 16:5-12). The problem with the Pharisees' teaching was that they taught dependence upon the world and the law. They failed to focus on the Kingdom of God.

Declaring To God Our Needs

The Pharisees only cared about the things of this world, recognition of men and wealth. Jesus taught his disciples that they were to first be concerned about what concerned their heavenly Father and not worry about the things of this world, because their names were written in heaven (Luke 10:20).

Unfortunately, most people follow the leaven (teaching) of the Pharisees as they seek the wealth of this world. Jesus warned his disciples about such a way of living. He rebuked the crowds because he knew that they followed him only to be fed. Rather than seeking that which would never perish, they coveted that which would perish every day (John 6:31-34). Every day, men and women expend their resources and energy seeking to obtain, while being afraid of losing that which will not last. In so doing, they fail to live for that which they can never lose.

Every relationship, accomplishment, and possession that men and women desire on earth will one day be lost. This is not a prophecy of doom, but the plain reality of our mortality. It is why we set up wills and trust funds. When our life ends here, we know what we have acquired will no longer be ours. We will be nothing more than a memory for our loved ones. This reality is not meant to be depressing, but should prompt us to seek that which we cannot lose, as Jesus instructed us. He taught his disciples to invest their lives in that which thieves cannot steal, rust cannot consume and moths cannot ruin (Matthew 6:19-21). Ultimately, Jesus is the only reason for living and the treasure that we will never lose. This is why Jesus referred to himself as the bread of life five times in his instruction to the people (John 6:35, 41, 50-51, 58). If they were seeking something to sustain their life, then Jesus, not loaves of bread, was the answer.

At the last supper, Jesus gave another spiritual meaning to bread. When Jesus took the bread and gave thanks, he gave it to his disciples and made a comparison to his body. The bread was to be a reminder of what Jesus accomplished for them on the

97

cross (Matthew 26:26). He would demonstrate his great love for us by laying down his life for us (John 15:13). Through his sacrifice, the way to the Father and the ability to pray as he taught in the Lord's prayer, would be possible. The Gospel of Matthew makes this abundantly clear when we read that the veil in the temple that separated the Holy of Holies was ripped down the middle from top to bottom. The Holy of Holies, from the time of Moses' construction of the tabernacle, represented the place where the presence of God was. From the time of Moses and the Tabernacle, God's presence was always separate from the people; only the high priest could enter once a year with a sacrifice of blood. When Jesus died, however, the way to the Father was open for all who believe in the name of Jesus (Matthew 27:51). While the declaration to God for our daily bread refers to physical sustenance in the Lord's Prayer, bread in the New Testament also has a worship component. In the early church, Luke identified four components of worship: apostolic teaching, fellowship, breaking of bread, and prayer (Acts 2:42). The breaking of bread (eating together), which probably also included a celebration of the Lord's Supper, was seen as distinct from teaching, fellowship and prayer, yet still an important aspect of worship. Today, worship particularly corporate worship, is understood to be something that is done weekly, typically Sunday morning, but in the early church it was a daily occurrence practiced both in the temple and in homes. In the homes, eating (breaking bread) was included again as part of worship (Acts 2:46). On the first day of the week, Luke says that the church in Troas gathered to "break bread", however, the context indicates that they had gathered to worship and to hear Paul's teaching (Acts 20:7, 11).

The connection between bread and worship is seen most clearly in descriptions of the Lord's Supper, where bread refers to the body of Jesus. As all those present share the bread and then the cup, this is a symbol of Christian unity in the body of Jesus, which Paul referred to as the church, while the cup represented his blood, shed to purchase our forgiveness in the sight of the Father (1 Corinthians 10:16-17). In recounting the establishment of the Lord's Supper, Paul reminded the Corinthians, that on that occasion, Jesus took bread and gave it to the disciples to share. Paul saw this symbol as a means to declare and remember the death of Jesus until he returns. Since the bread referred to Jesus' body and was a sign of unity within the church, treating the Lord's Supper without proper respect was a serious offense (1 Corinthians 11:23-28). For this reason, Paul taught that each person was to examine himself.

Again, Paul linked worship and bread when he reminded the Corinthians that the same God who supplies our bodies with physical bread will also provide a harvest of righteousness to believers (2 Corinthians 9:10). Bread, therefore, was a symbol of physical nourishment, for which we were to go to God, but it was also a picture of spiritual growth leading to the righteousness of Jesus being produced in our life.

The New Testament teaching on breaking the bread was foreshadowed in the Old Testament by the practice of the priests who ate what was called shewbread. These twelve loaves of bread were set out each week before the Lord, but at the end of the week, the priests and only the priests ate this bread (Leviticus 24:5-9; Hebrews 9:2). In Jesus, all followers are priests, not only a special group of people as in the Old Testament. Therefore, every believer has the right to take part in eating the bread in the Lord's Supper.

Sharing a meal

Even though bread had a powerful spiritual meaning, it also is seen in a practical, life-sustaining manner. Jesus would sit down with friends and family and share bread together. In this sense, it means that he would share a meal with them (Mark

Declaring To God Our Needs

3:20; Luke 14:1). The concept of bread also was expanded to refer to supplying a person's living needs. Paul reminded the Thessalonians that he did not eat anyone's bread while he was there, but he provided for his own needs. In this case, bread refers to more than physical bread, but to the needs a person has to live (2 Thessalonians 3:8, 12). Paul made this point so that others would follow his example and not live off the hard work of others.

One final observation before we move on to the next prayer declaration. Jesus told us to go to Father for our "daily" bread. For most of us living in the affluent west, we already have our daily bread waiting for us in the kitchen. We are so wealthy that we do not need to depend on Father every day to sustain us. With this declaration, Jesus reminded his disciples of their daily dependence upon Father. This command reminds us of what the children of Israel experienced in the wilderness. Each morning, they depended upon the manna arriving. They received one day's ration and no more except on Friday, when the manna collected would last until the manna returned Sunday morning, skipping the Sabbath (Saturday).

Have you ever pondered how you would respond if God chose to give to you what you needed only one day at a time? Many of us have no concern for today's bread, or even tomorrow's; we are concerned about our bread when we reach retirement, or when our children begin college. We are a future oriented people who in many ways have forgotten to live in daily dependence upon our loving Father. Jesus reminded his disciples that if they did not become like little children, they would never enter into the Kingdom of Heaven (Luke 18:17). Children, cared for in their father's home, own nothing themselves. They have no concern for what the family does or doesn't have. They care not for what the family financial reserves are. They only know that when they need something, they go to mom or dad for what they need. This is the type of prayer Jesus taught his disciples to declare to Father. They were not to be anxious about today's bread, tomorrow's bread, or their future bread. All worry about the future was illegal because they had an all powerful Father who would give them what they needed when they needed it.

The Apostle Paul went even further. He taught us to continue to trust, even when we lack provision. To the Philippians, he declared that he had learned to be content in plenty and in want (Philippians 4:12-13). Paul grasped an important secret that David had written in the Psalms (Psalm 16:15-18). David delighted because the Lord was his inheritance. Paul had learned that same principle. He no longer needed his daily bread to be content, because every day he had Jesus. When we can learn to live in peace and rest, even when we experience need, we have learned a powerful way to live.

The New Testament teaching on bread indicates that this command refers to more than just physical needs. Following the Lord's Prayer in Matthew, Jesus taught that to those who seek the Kingdom and its righteousness, all their physical needs would be met (Matthew 6:33). In the wilderness, Jesus defeated Satan's temptation by reminding him that man does not live by bread alone but by every word that proceeds from the mouth of God. Finally, Jesus revealed himself to be the bread of life. Therefore, our command for bread must be more than physical bread, but a sustaining and life-giving revelation of Jesus, who is the true manna that descended from heaven.

Summary

Jesus instructed his followers to declare to God their needs to sustain their life. As in the previous declarations, Jesus taught his disciples to approach the Father boldly with commands. Although this approach may seem inappropriate, we have to recognize that this is what Jesus taught us. If Jesus had wanted

Declaring To God Our Needs

to soften them to mere requests, another form could have been used, but Jesus used this strong "command" quite likely to remind us of the authority and closeness that the Father has given to us, along with God's revelation as man's helper. Jesus taught us to address our need boldly to the Father for bread.

Since "bread" is used in the New Testament for more than physical needs, it is likely that Jesus meant for us to go to the Father for not only what we need physically, but also spiritually and emotionally. Since Jesus declared himself several times in John 6 to be the bread of life, our declaration for bread could also refer to our needing the continual presence of Jesus in our life through the Holy Spirit (Luke 11:13), to sustain us spiritually and emotionally.

In the Old Testament, men like Abraham and Moses boldly made assertions to God. In the case of Moses, Scripture informs us that God changed his mind due to his bold prayer. As followers of Jesus, we are in an even more intimate relationship with Father than either Abraham and Moses were. While they never had the privilege to refer to God as "Father", we've been commanded to speak to him in that way. This means that not only can we approach God with the same boldness as Abraham or Moses, but that we can be as bold with Father as Jesus was, because he has given to us the right to be called children of God. To lack boldness with Father indicates a hesitancy on our part to enter into a close relationship with Him. We assume that if Moses had not interceded for Israel, God would have destroyed them, just like He destroyed Sodom, because not even ten righteous men could be found. Thus, not to make bold affirmations and declarations to Father means we may not see and experience what God is willing to do for us.

102

Declaring To God Our Needs

Questions for Reflection

1. What do you find are the implications of issuing a personal command to Almighty God?

2. What would be your emotional response if you had to trust Father for the provision of your meal each morning?

3. Reflect on how Father has sustained your life through spiritual means.

Papa, my life is completely dependent upon your provision for me. I depend upon you to provide everything I need. It is an illusion for me to think that I acquire anything by means of my own efforts. I seek from you that which I need for my physical life as I receive from you the strength and grace to seek the kingdom and righteousness. May my heart not be distracted from you my Provider and begin to worry about what might happen tomorrow, for today you promise to provide for everything that I need. Amen.

Chapter 7
Calling On God's Forgiveness According To Our Own
Matthew 6:12

After expressing a command that God fulfill His promise to take care of our physical, spiritual and emotional needs, Jesus instructed his disciples to issue a command for forgiveness. However, Jesus instructed us to issue the command as a condition. We claim Father's forgiveness to the extent that we practice forgiveness ourselves. Man is completely dependent upon God for both his physical and spiritual needs. He is not autonomous from God; he depends each day for God to supply his needs. Jesus' instruction reminds man of his dependent relationship. It is a sin for man to think he is independent from God's providing care. Without the bread that God supplies, man dies physically. Without the forgiveness that Father supplies through Jesus' death on the cross, man will forever exist as spiritually dead, separated from Him. On several occasions, Jesus taught that our forgiveness of others was a necessary response to Father's forgiveness of us.

As we meet and work with struggling Christians, it is not unusual to find that at the core of their struggle, are issues of unforgiveness. To put it another way, it is not unusual to discover that people who are struggling relationally or have powerful addictions in their life, also have struggles with unforgiveness in their life. Those observations underscore the importance that Jesus placed on forgiveness, not only our forgiveness by the Father, but also the Christian's commitment to forgive those who have hurt him.

In his teaching on forgiveness, Jesus explained why. This fifth command/declaration to God is unique from all others, because it is expressed as a condition. The previous declarations do not depend on anything. God's name is always holy. His Kingdom is to come and His will to be done. We need not do anything else to receive our daily bread but declare it. Forgiveness, though, is dependent upon something we must do first.

More than anything else, a lack of forgiveness prevents men and women who claim to follow Jesus from experiencing the freedom for which Jesus died (Galatians 5:1). It is strange to observe how many people will go to Bible school, serve in the church, serve and give to the poor, but stumble over the command to forgive those who have hurt them. In each and every case, that individual fails to experience the joy of living which Jesus desires to give to them, while all their service is only a reflection of obligation and duty. Often, it is fear which holds them back. Fear that if they forgive, they will be hurt again. Strangely, they hurt themselves more by refusing to forgive, than the possibility of being hurt if they did forgive. Ironically, the belief that unforgiveness is protection is quite the opposite, because we live in a fallen and broken world in which people get hurt whether they forgive or not.

At other times, individuals deceive themselves into thinking that if they forgive someone who hurt them, then they are justifying the wrong committed against them. Nothing could be further from the truth. When we forgive, we release the bonds in our own spirit that keeps us chained to the hurt and bitterness that we've endured since the moment we were hurt. Jesus tells us to forgive others, not for the person who offended us, but to free ourselves!

Jesus commands forgiveness, not to place us in danger, but because the decision to forgive will open floodgates of freedom in our lives. Many people either refuse to believe that truth or outright deny it. Fear enslaves them and deceives them from taking such a major step toward freedom. For them, following Jesus is not really a joy, but an endless list of rules to keep as they try various means to remove the pain of hurt. Some resort to addictive behaviors in order to medicate the pain that they feel from the hurt they've endured and compounded by their refusal to forgive. Others seek out relationships with people they think can make a difference in their life. Almost always, they are disappointed, because the person from whom they seek love is often as needy as they are. For them, Christianity is more of a prison, because they have not experienced the power of Jesus to set them free.

Forgive

The word "forgive" refers to removal or cancellation of a debt. Forgiveness is when God removes the weight of sin from us. God lifts off the burden of our sin. The word can be used in a business or financial sense. To forgive means to cancel a debt. The Bible teaches that the debtor is a slave to the creditor. We are in debt to God, but because of Jesus' death on the cross, our debt is removed. Just as the cancellation of a financial debt removes a burden from us, so also we feel a burden lifted when we experience God's forgiveness in our life. The lifting off of sin frees us from sin's consequences and places us in a position where we can address Father. Because of the word's underlying meaning to "lift off," or "to leave," the word has a wide range of meanings, one of which refers to Father's canceling our "sin debt" to Him.

Forgiveness and bread emphasize our need for God. As bread addresses a physical need that our bodies require, so also forgiveness provides that which our spirits need to thrive. Forgiveness is compared to being freed or loosed. A sin or debt holds us in bondage; being forgiven is being freed from a burden. The master reminded the wicked servant that he had forgiven him all his debts, only on the basis of asking him. However, the wicked servant came under judgment because of his failure to exercise the same mercy to his fellow servant. The

107

Calling On God's Forgiveness According To Our Own

judgment upon the wicked servant was torment. Surprisingly, Jesus said that Father would put a person who refuses to practice forgiveness in torment until he learns to forgive from the heart (Matthew 18:27, 32, 35).

The action of the wicked servant is a reminder of those who struggle to accept Father's forgiveness in the first place. Since the wicked servant had been forgiven, he had absolutely no reason to force his fellow servant to pay his debt to him, unless, however, the wicked servant's pride drove him to think that he could still pay the debt for which he had been forgiven. It is clear from Jesus' words that the wicked servant had no comprehension of the magnitude of his debt because he did not ask to be forgiven, but to have the time to pay it back. The master graciously gave the wicked servant that which he should have asked for, forgiveness. When we refuse to accept Father's forgiveness from our hearts, then we will likely struggle with forgiving those who have hurt us, because our hearts are still hard. Due to Jesus' words, it is not surprising that people who refuse to forgive live in torment. These tormented individuals may spend a fortune in counseling and therapy with little or no improvement other than gaining a few skills to manage their addictions and struggles. Jesus declared that it is absolutely necessary to practice forgiveness in order to be forgiven by Father.

We forgive and are forgiven

While the previous declarations were unconditional with no qualifications attached, to be forgiven includes a condition, as we have forgiven those who have sinned against us. This qualification is in perfect agreement with what Jesus taught about forgiveness; it always assumes the result that we who have already been forgiven will practice forgiveness of others. To be unforgiving toward others reveals a rejection of what Father has freely offered to us (Matthew 6:12, 14, 15; Luke 11:4). This is actually a prayer of great courage, because it declares to Father that we have forgiven all that those have done against us, so that we are free to be completely forgiven by Father.

Why is this so? After teaching the disciples about prayer, Jesus declared that forgiveness is a condition of being forgiven. Without forgiving others, we cut ourselves from Father's forgiveness. In other words, practicing forgiveness is a sign of conversion, being born again, being a new creature and a partaker of the divine nature. If we refuse to forgive, we reveal that our nature has not been changed. It is Father's nature to forgive, while it is man's nature not to forgive. Throughout Scripture, God consistently forgives those who repent and seek mercy. However, it is man's nature to hang onto a grudge and seek vindication.

On other occasions, Jesus taught further about forgiveness. Still assuming the law, Peter asked Jesus how often he should forgive his brother who continued to sin against him (Matthew 18:21; Luke 17:3, 4). In his response, Jesus taught that forgiveness is to know no bounds. Our heavenly Father has so freely forgiven us, not only canceling our debt, but paying our debt himself so that justice might not be ignored. When we forgive those who sin against us, we turn our debt over to Father for his attention and action. Our forgiveness of others, is actually a reflection of how much we have learned to trust Father. Not only are we to forgive so that we will be forgiven, but Jesus also indicated that a lack of forgiveness will block Father from even hearing our prayers. Refusing to forgive cuts off our ability to communicate with Father (Mark 11:25, 26). Again, it is not surprising that those who struggle with unforgiveness seem to lack God's power in their life, suffering from depression and loneliness. While they may say prayers, Jesus warns them that their refusal to forgive prevents them from being heard.

Jesus forgave sins

Not only did Jesus instruct his followers, but he practiced forgiveness himself and in so doing he revealed himself to be God (Matthew 9:2, 5, 6; Mark 2:5, 7, 9, 10; Luke 5:20, 21, 23, 24). Jesus declared to a paralytic that his sins were forgiven; when he did so they were lifted off. Since Jesus is God, he gave us an example for how we are to forgive. The paralytic was responsible to Jesus for his sins. Jesus canceled the man's debt toward him and removed the burden forever. As the scribes correctly understood, by declaring the man's sins forgiven, Jesus revealed himself to be God, because only God had the authority to forgive sins in that manner.

Men can forgive that which is done directly against them, but Jesus did more. He made an unqualified statement of forgiveness covering not only a possible sin that this man may have committed against Jesus, but all sin that this man had ever committed. Only God could authoritatively make such a statement. Jesus' declaration became an opportunity for him to demonstrate that he clearly had the authority to forgive sins and in so doing reveal that he was God. By restoring the man's ability to walk, which no one could do without God's power, Jesus revealed his authority to forgive. Anyone can declare sins to be forgiven, but only a person with power can restore to a paralytic the ability to walk and, therefore, forgive sins as well.

On another occasion, Jesus revealed himself as a prophet to confirm his authority to forgive sins. With the sinful woman, Jesus declared her sins forgiven and instructed her to go in peace (Luke 7:47, 48, 49). The Pharisee had already questioned Jesus' behavior by thinking that Jesus could not be a prophet and allow such a sinful woman to touch him (Luke 7:39). Jesus revealed how the disreputable, sinful woman had treated him with more hospitality and respect than the respectable Pharisee had (Luke 7:40-46). In so doing, Jesus revealed that he was a prophet, because he knew that the Pharisee questioned whether Jesus could be a prophet without being told. Jesus went on to make an obvious point that the Pharisee should have understood without Jesus pointing it out. Jesus forgave the sins of the woman, explaining to the Pharisee that those of whom much has been forgiven, love much. Even after all this, others at the table criticized Jesus because they didn't believe he had the power to forgive sins. In this story, we find a contrast with the wicked servant spoken of in the parable. The woman accepted her forgiveness and expressed love toward Jesus. The wicked servant was forgiven, but didn't express love, indicating that he had failed to accept the forgiveness offered to him.

The clearest example of Jesus showing us how to forgive was when he forgave those who were executing him (Luke 23:34). Not only did he forgive them, but he understood their problem; they were blind to what they were doing. This did not mean that they didn't know what they were doing, because the Roman soldiers were experts at execution. It also did not mean that they were not responsible for what they were doing. They were completely responsible for the sin of crucifying Jesus, an innocent man. They did not know what they were doing because they failed to grasp the significance of their actions. From their perspective they were following orders without considering the immorality of what they were doing by crucifying their Savior and creator. What makes this episode so powerful is that in previous examples, Jesus was functioning as God when forgiving sins. Here, Jesus is placed in the exact position that we face when we too forgive. Although Jesus was innocent, the Roman soldiers were causing Jesus great pain, yet he forgave them. As God, Jesus could have rightfully exercised judgment against them, but he responded with love. This is the exact model that Jesus calls his followers to practice.

111

Disciples' authority to forgive sins

Not only did Jesus forgive sins, but he made a surprising statement to his disciples regarding forgiveness. Jesus told his disciples that if they declared others forgiven of their sin then the sins would be forgiven, but if they did not declare forgiveness, the sins would remain (John 20:23). In this way, Jesus gave to his disciples an authority similar to his own. As already seen, when Jesus forgave the paralytic and the sinful woman, he revealed his authority to forgive sin, but here he gave a surprisingly similar authority to the disciples. Furthermore, Jesus gave the disciples authority to retain sins. This could not regard sins committed directly against the disciples, because in that case Jesus would be contradicting the command that he had already given for the disciples to forgive all sins committed against them. This statement only makes sense in parallel to Jesus' own authority to forgive sins as Father and Jesus do. It is such a surprising statement that it is hard to conceive of Jesus uttering it.

Jesus' words give us another glimpse into the significance of the Spirit's indwelling presence in our life. The Spirit clearly has the authority to forgive sin. Since he dwells in each and every believer, he has the power to reveal to that believer what needs to be done with the individual's sin. This statement is similar to what Jesus said to Peter, that the keys to the kingdom have been given to him. This seems to be more than just proclaiming the gospel (Matthew 16:19).

The Roman Catholic Church teaches that when a priest absolves sin in the confessional, the condemnation of sin (mortal sin) is removed. Through penance, the temporal (venial) aspect of sin must be paid for by the Christian. While we would not agree with the Roman Catholic Church's view on penance removing the temporal punishment of sin, Roman Catholicism does take Jesus' words seriously.

Calling On God's Forgiveness According To Our Own

The authority to remove and retain sins reflects on who we are in Jesus. Scripture tells us that we are in Christ. We are co-heirs with him, children of Abba Father, who have been made partakers of the divine nature. Jesus' delegation of authority over sin is a natural implication of who he has made us to be.

Of course, the disciples were not given the authority to use this power in any way that might contradict the way Jesus used it. Disciples are to use this authority in line with the Spirit's direction as he dwells with them and leads them into all truth. It seems that in giving this command, Jesus is installing his followers as his representatives on earth. Prior to making this statement, Jesus had given this disciples the Holy Spirit, who led Jesus continually throughout his life on the earth.

Jesus' statement seems to be a precursor to the Great Commission. At that time, Jesus gave the disciples responsibility to make disciples, but here he seems to be giving them the power and authority to do so in his name. In 2 Corinthians 5, Paul declared that followers of Jesus are ambassadors of the kingdom. In that role, believers act on earth in Jesus' place and with Jesus' authority. It is the believer's responsibility to declare the sins of those who repent to be forgiven in Jesus name, just as Jesus would if he were present.

Two stories from Acts reveal the authority that the apostles received and practiced regarding sinful behavior. In Acts 5 is the account of Ananias and and his wife, Sapphira, who lied about the sale price of their field. When Ananias brought the offering, Peter exposed his deceit, at which point Ananias fell dead. Three hours Sapphira showed up. Peter asked her if the amount that Ananias had claimed was the sale price. When she said yes, confirming her cooperation with the lie, Peter declared that she too would die in her sin. In this case, we see a fulfillment of what Jesus declared in John 20:23. Jesus gave the apostles the authority to forgive sin or retain sins of another. Peter did not

declare forgiveness, but declared that the sin of Ananias and
Sapphira remained

Forgiveness defined and described

While Jesus freely forgave sin, he revealed that there was
one sin or action that would never be forgiven. When Jesus
made this statement, he didn't clearly identify what that sin was.
Consequently, today there is disagreement as to what that sin is.
Some declare that it is a lifelong refusal to believe the gospel.
However, this conclusion does not explain how this is a sin
against the Holy Spirit and not against Jesus, in whom
unbelieving men have failed to place their trust (Matthew 12:31,
32; Mark 3:28; Luke 12:10). Others view Jesus' words in the
context of what the Pharisees were claiming. They had just
attributed to Satan Jesus' power of delivering people from
demons. Jesus clearly showed that he was operating according
to the Holy Spirit, because Satan's kingdom could never stand if
Satan were fighting against himself as the Pharisees implied.
While the Pharisees did reveal great unbelief, they went beyond
unbelief and identified God the Holy Spirit with Satan. Jesus
declared that this action would not be forgiven. A person who
cannot recognize the Holy Spirit as coming from God, but
concludes him to be a deceiver, is truly lost. Such an individual
rejects the very person whose role is to lead men into a
relationship with Jesus. Without the presence of the Holy Spirit,
no man can come to faith in Jesus (Romans 8:9).

On another occasion, Jesus reminded his disciples of the
great blessing they had received (Mark 4:12). By following
Jesus and listening to his teaching, the disciples learned the
mysteries of the kingdom of heaven. The disciples not only
heard Jesus teach, but also heard his explanation of the parables.
Jesus revealed to his disciples that he spoke parables to separate
those who believed from those who refused to seek

understanding. Those who pursued the parable's meaning rather than concluding it was not worth the effort, received forgiveness from Jesus because they entered into a faith relationship with him.

When Simon requested to purchase the ability to impart the Holy Spirit to others, Peter rebuked him by telling him to repent so that the Lord would forgive him. Peter's words to Simon revealed that for Simon to receive forgiveness, he needed to repent or to change his manner of thinking (Acts 8:22). In Romans, Paul writes that those who have received forgiveness have received blessing from Jesus (Romans 4:7). In quoting Psalm 32:1, Paul included the concept that forgiveness meant our sin is covered. In this one verse, the New Testament teaching of removing our sin and the Old Testament teaching of our sin being covered are both illustrated.

James merged the physical and spiritual in the concept of forgiveness. Those who are sick, literally weak, are to call the elders of the church to come and pray over them. James promised that the prayer offered in faith will restore the sick as well as lead to forgiveness if sin is involved (James 5:14-15). James explained that all believers are to confess their sin to one another in order to be healed (James 5:16). The James 5 passage merges the concepts of forgiveness, prayer and physical healing. In his teaching, James expands prayer for healing from the apostles, to the elders, and then to all believers. In these verses, James helps us understand that we are whole beings. Body, soul and spirit cannot be separated; rather they influence one another. Physical healing can come through prayer and confession, as does forgiveness of sin. As people created in the image of God, we are so interconnected in our being that we cannot easily define where the impact of the body ends and where that of the spirit and soul begins. John confirmed the importance of confession when he declared that through confession we are forgiven and cleansed from our unrighteousness caused by sin (1

John 1:9). A little later, John reminded his readers that because of Jesus, our sins are forgiven (1 John 2:12). Our sins are no longer associated with us, because they have been removed from us. David declared, in the Old Testament that as far as the east is from the west, our sins have been removed (forgiven, lifted off) from us (Psalm 103:12).

Debts

The New Testament compares our sin to a debt. It is primarily a debt that we have before God. For this reason, after committing adultery with Bathsheba and orchestrating her husband Uriah's death, David declared to God that against Him alone he had sinned (Psalm 51:4). With the gravity of David's sin against Uriah, it surprises us to read David's words, but David understood that sin was primarily an action against heaven, because David belonged to God as did Bathsheba and Uriah. Through his offenses, he sinned primarily against God (Psalm 51:4).

Since sin is primarily an offense against God, Jesus instructed his disciples to declare that God forgive them (Matthew 6:12) in the same manner that they forgive those who have hurt them. However, in the prayer declaration, Jesus did not use the word "sin", but the word "debts." Our sin makes us debtors before God and to each other. We have a debt to pay, but we are incapable of paying that debt and are helpless unless God removes it through forgiveness. This is why forgiving others is so necessary, because if we fail to forgive those who have such a small debt toward us, then how can we expect God to forgive our unpayable debt toward him?

Summary

All the previous declarations have been in a command form,

as in declarations for God's name to be made holy, his kingdom to come and his will to be done. These three were followed by the direct declaration made for God to supply what is needed for life. However, this declaration to be forgiven was given with a qualification that we would also forgive others. Like the previous declarations, this one to be forgiven in command form is dependent upon our fulfilling the prerequisite of practicing forgiveness on our own part. It is as if this part of the prayer is like a contract with stipulations before the contract can be fulfilled. If the stipulations are not fulfilled, the agreement is null and void.

The topic of forgiveness reveals another example of Jesus' teaching, that unless we become like children, we will never enter the kingdom of heaven. Children respond to hurt very differently than others who are older. When a small child gets hurt while playing with other children, he or she goes to a person in authority: mommy, daddy, or a teacher. In tears, the child explains what happened. The adult provides comfort and reassures the child that everything will be alright so that the child can go back and play. In a few minutes, the child is playing even with the one who hurt them as if nothing had happened. In the Garden of Gethsemane, Jesus modeled this childlike approach. As we've already seen, Mark 14 reveals that this is the only time in the Gospels that Jesus addresses Father as "Abba Father," which in English could be translated as "daddy" or "papa." In Jesus' prayer, he has become like a small child enduring the pain of his life, seeking comfort from his daddy. As we grow older, we tend to share our hurt with others, who may sympathize, but cannot provide us with the comfort and assurance that we need. We may never go to our Abba Father for the comfort and assurance to know that everything will be alright so that we can go back "to play" free from hurt. We may even conclude that Father abandoned us in our time of need. Therefore, we return with damaged relationships and our guard up.

Calling On God's Forgiveness According To Our Own

Questions for Reflection

1. How do you view the role of forgiveness in your relationship with Jesus?

2. In what way would you explain to a child the importance of forgiveness?

3. Consider those hurts that you find difficult to forgive. Why do you think those particular hurts are difficult for you?

4. In what ways can you remind yourself to go to Abba Father with your hurts, rather than telling others about who has hurt you?

Papa, Jesus' instruction to declare your forgiveness as I forgive pushes me to allow your Spirit to examine my heart so that I am not harboring any bitterness against anyone. More than anything, I desire to have nothing hindering my relationship with you. I hunger to be completely forgiven by you and live in the full freedom for which Jesus died and gave to me. Then I ask you to reveal to me any hidden areas of unforgiveness lurking in my heart; so that I might repent, forgive, and be set free. Amen.

Chapter 8
Our Request To God
Matthew 6:13

Preparation is key to any endeavor. Several years ago, I planned to take a long bike ride with several friends. Over a year before the trip, I had ridden many miles, but during the last year I had ridden little. I suspected that I might not be prepared for the ride which would take us over the coastal range from Portland to the Pacific coast. Because I had just begun a new job and was busy, I did not pay attention to that nagging suspicion that I should prepare more. When the day of the ride came, we set out. Things began well, but as we neared the summit, my legs started to cramp, requiring me to walk out the cramps. The rest of the day was a physical challenge for me. What should have been great enjoyment if I had been better prepared, became a physical burden. Recognizing the need to prepare for a physical challenge is important. Recognizing a warning to prepare for a spiritual challenge is even more important.

Of all the topics mentioned in the Lord's Prayer, this is the only one that is not formed as a command in the original Greek language, although it is translated as a command in English. In Greek it is written grammatically as a request. There exists a simple explanation for its differentiation from previous commands. If it had been given as a negative command in Greek, the meaning would have been "stop leading us into temptation." Since Father does not lead us into temptation, a prayer requesting that he stop doing so would be inaccurate and inappropriate. This explains the difference in grammatical form, because Father does not tempt us.

Temptation understood as examination

This prayer raised another question. We know that God cannot be tempted and does not tempt us (James 1:13). If temptation has nothing to do with God, why would Jesus tell us

119

to pray that Father not lead us into it? In response, our request seems more in line with asking Father to lead us through and out of temptation along the lines of what Paul wrote in 1 Corinthians 10:13. When we are tempted Father shows us a way through the temptation.

The Greek word "peirazo" translated as "tempted" has a basic meaning of "examine." This is important to remember because the same Greek word is translated into English using several words. When the word refers to Satan's activity, the word is translated as "tempt." However, when the word is used of God's activity the word is translated as "test." This requires some explanation. The essence of Satan's temptation is an examination with the intent to bring about failure. This was Satan's intent when he attacked Job. He tempted Job to curse God. If Job had cursed God, it is certain that Satan would have followed up with condemnation of Job. However, when Father "tests" us, his intent is not our failure. Rather Father tests expecting us to pass and to approve us. In other words, when Father desires to give us a promotion, he tests us. Again this is what happened to Job. At the end of Job, God promoted him, by giving to Job an increased revelation for which Job praised God (Job 42:5). Previously Job had heard of God, but after his encounter his eyes had seen him. Even though all of Job's losses were restored, his greatest gift what an increased revelation of God.

In the Garden of Gethsemane, Jesus instructed his disciples to watch and pray that they might not fall into temptation because the spirit is willing but the flesh is weak (Matthew 26:41). Earlier that evening, Jesus had warned Peter that Peter would deny him. Peter refused to heed Jesus' warning. When Jesus told Peter and the other disciples to pray so that they would not fall into temptation, Peter failed to grasp the connection with what Jesus said earlier and so he fell back asleep. Later that night, Peter fulfilled exactly what Jesus had said he would do and what Peter denied that he would do. Temptation overcame Peter, who failed to pray so that he would not fall into temptation. Actually, Peter's failure was not when he denied Jesus; it occurred earlier in the evening when he failed to believe Jesus' warning. If Peter had taken to heart what Jesus had said, then he would have been so distraught that he could not have slept in the Garden. Jesus was just as tired as the disciples, probably more so, but he could not sleep, because he believed the prophetic declarations in Isaiah 53 about the suffering he would endure. Had Peter prayed and asked Father for the strength not to deny Jesus, Father would have surely spared Peter the agony of denying Jesus whom he loved.

Peter's failure reminds us of an important truth. We can be tempted and fall even in areas that are strengths in our life. For Peter, his love of Jesus was an area of strength. Jesus pointed this out when he restored Peter in John 21; three times he asked Peter if he loved him. In the end, Peter responded that Jesus knew Peter loved him. These questions were not for Jesus' information, but for Peter to have an opportunity to confess what Jesus knew to be true. Jesus was drawing out and revealing the truth of Peter's love for Jesus during a time when Peter may have doubted it after his denial.

Peter's actions when the soldiers came to arrest Jesus may have caused Peter to conclude that he had demonstrated his love for Jesus. While the other disciples held back, Peter pulled his sword and went after those seeking to arrest Jesus. Scripture tells us that a cohort came to arrest Jesus. A Roman cohort was made up of six hundred trained Roman soldiers. These trained men could do a lot of damage, particularly to an untrained fisherman wielding a sword. If Jesus had not intervened, Peter likely would have been killed for nothing, because Jesus had already shown that he needed no defending. When he asked who the soldiers sought, Jesus responded with the Holy Name of God, "I am," and the soldiers all fell back (John 18:6). While foolish,

Our Request To God

Peter's actions revealed his love and commitment to Jesus. One of the times when we are at risk of temptation is when we believe we've had success or proven our point. After attacking with the sword, Peter may have concluded that he had shown Jesus he was willing to die for him, but Peter didn't realize his test was still to come.

I remember a pastor, who had fallen to temptation, share that he fell in an area which he considered a strength in his life. Since it was a strength, the pastor had not guarded it. He warned about the danger of an "unguarded strength." After Peter confronted the soldiers, he may have let his guard down so that when the servant girl asked if he was a follower of Jesus, Peter's fatigue and confusion got the best of him and he uttered words that he never believed would ever come out of his mouth. Peter's example reminds us of the wisdom in Proverbs 4:23, to guard our heart, for it is the wellspring of our life.

Jesus' instruction to pray that Father not lead us into temptation seems to be a recognition of our weak flesh and our need for Father's help to overcome. If Jesus who had never sinned felt the need to pray in the Garden to prepare himself for his ordeal and not fall to temptation, how much more should we, who have experience with sin, do the same? Without His help, we are likely to follow the example of Cain. God had warned Cain that sin was crouching at his door, but he must overcome it (Genesis 4:7). God's words indicate that Cain was being tempted to do evil, but God also implied that Cain was able to overcome that temptation. Tragically, he did not overcome, but succumbed. As a result, Abel's life ended and Cain's was forever altered.

Temptation's solution

Overcoming temptation is more than taking a passive

122

Our Request To God

approach; it requires that we take action to overcome the temptation. Jesus commanded his disciples to watch, stay alert, and pray so that they would not fall into temptation. Jesus reminded them that the spirit of man is willing to obey, but his flesh is weak (Matthew 26:41; Mark 14:38; Luke 22:40, 46). This verse reveals the battle that wages inside man, between the spirit that desires to follow God and the flesh that demands we follow its desires. With Jesus' death on the cross, his resurrection and the coming of the Holy Spirit, Paul reveals that the flesh no longer has the power it once had. In Romans 6, Paul taught that the old nature, the flesh, was crucified with Jesus on the cross (Romans 6:5-7). In Romans 8, Paul reminded the Romans that they were no longer in the flesh, but in the Spirit (Romans 8:9). Does Paul mean that we are no longer tempted? Of course not! Even though our flesh has died with Jesus and the believer has been freed from condemnation, every believer still has a memory of the power of the flesh. These memories can become the new source of temptation for the believer. In any case, Jesus taught that prayer was an important component in defeating temptation. Prayer functions to renew our mind to Heaven's reality countering the temptation to be conformed to the world (Romans 12:1-2). As Jesus taught in the Lord's Prayer, we need God's help to overcome temptation through prayer.

In the Parable of the Sower, Jesus compared the Kingdom of God to a garden. In the Kingdom, there are several challenges to our life with Jesus. If our heart is hard toward spiritual things, then we are blind to the Kingdom, like the seed that fell on the path. Those who are blind to God are so because Satan blinds those who are perishing (2 Corinthians 4:4).

With those who are not blind, but only weak, Satan uses temptation. The seed that fell on rocky soil grew up quickly, but got burned up because of a lack of depth and strength under the strong summer sun (Luke 8:13). Spiritually, it is succumbing to temptation that causes the withering of spiritual life. We

123

succumb because we have failed to grasp the superiority and joy of following God. Rather than holding onto the promise for what is better, we give in to a short term gratification, hoping to meet our needs. The things of the world still appear attractive and beautiful in our sight, because they give us temporary joy. When we mature to the point that we can see that everything the Father offers through Jesus far surpasses anything we could possibly acquire in this world; we resist the temptation to gain what is superior. When we are so captivated with love and worship of God, Satan has nothing with which to tempt us, because he will never tempt us with a closer relationship with God.

Satan may try to deceive us into thinking that the world has a means of drawing us into a closer relationship with Father, which Jesus addresses with the third defective soil. The seed that falls among the weeds gets choked out because of the power of the weeds. Spiritually, Jesus referred to the things of this world that distract the individual from the things of Father by deceiving him to think that love of the world can lead us to God, or that we can both love the world and the Kingdom, which Jesus declared was impossible. The fact is that things of the world are attractive and they do offer some enjoyment. If the world was the spiritual equivalent of eating vegetables, no one would be tempted. At the time of this writing I am fifty-five years old. In those years, I have never been tempted by brussel sprouts. There is a good reason for that; I have no affection for them. However, I do have affection for coffee and dark chocolate. Like coffee and dark chocolate, the world offers dessert for our eyes and desires; hence we are tempted.

What we fail to grasp is that the Kingdom offers a better solution; if we wait a bit longer, we will be rewarded. We also get tripped up because we are all familiar with the advantages and pleasures the world has to offer, whereas we have never completely experienced the joys of the Kingdom. We are required to trust the good word of Father. However, if we doubt His goodness and love, then we may also doubt the beauty of the Kingdom and be tempted all the more to follow the world. We become like children who are offered a candy bar in the store. We can accept the candy, or we can trust our Father's word that he has a much better gift for us as home. If the child trusts his father, the candy bar will not tempt him much, but if the child questions his father's judgment regarding surprises, then he will play it safe and choose the candy bar, only to shed tears when he finds out what he missed at home.

Although temptations always have a certain power, Father has not left us without defense. He has given us two weapons with which we can overcome temptation. First, we are never the only person to experience the specific temptation that we face. Always there is someone else who went before us, who encountered what we face and who overcame it. Paul explained to the Corinthians that there is no temptation unique to us (1 Corinthians 10:13), but that others have faced it as well. Satan seeks to deceive us into thinking that we are the only ones facing our own particular situation, which renders us first, hopeless, and second, alone. Since we believe we are alone, we keep our struggle silent from others who could help us through their experience and victory over that temptation. In that case the power of the temptation is magnified in our eyes and appears more ominous than it really is. However, if we understand that others have gone before us, then we can observe how they defeated the temptation and follow their example.

Our second weapon lies with Father himself. Paul told the Corinthians that with every temptation, God our Father promises a way through it. Scripture tells us that Jesus faced every temptation known to man and defeated each one because he remained without sin (Hebrews 4:15-16). That means that Jesus is the expert at defeating temptation; all we need to do is go to him and learn how to defeat the temptation that faces us.

Our Request To God

Because Jesus has defeated all temptation, we can approach the throne of grace with confidence, knowing that from him, we will receive exactly what we need to defeat temptation and sin.

Even when we fall into temptation, we have resources at our disposal. Paul instructed the Galatians to gently restore those who have fallen into temptation and sin (Galatians 6:1). The fact that we can be restored is never an excuse to fall into sin, but it does offer help when we are struggling to mature to the point where we can overcome temptation. We don't have to give up and be filled with shame because of our inadequacies. There is another benefit in gently restoring those who have fallen; Paul taught that by doing this, we also avoid temptation. As we help others recover from having succumbed to temptation and first hand observe their pain, we can see through the deception of temptation and avoid it ourselves. We receive motivation because we do not want to experience the same pain and suffering our friend must endure while he is being restored.

Satan's temptation of Jesus

So that we can better understand Satan's tactics, Scripture includes Satan's temptation of Jesus. Along with Adam and Eve's failure in the Garden of Eden, Job's trial orchestrated by Satan and Peter's being sifted, this is one of the few recorded accounts of Satan seeking to tempt someone. Through Jesus' temptation, we learn some important principles in defeating it.

Temptation is not something that we should fear. The Holy Spirit led Jesus into the desert to be tempted (Matthew 4:1, 3; Mark 1:13; Luke 4:2). What the Spirit did is something that Jesus' teaching on prayer implies will not happen to us if we ask for deliverance. In other words, the Spirit led Jesus into the desert to be tempted in order to accomplish a specific purpose which is not applicable to us. We ask the Father not to lead us

126

into temptation, and so He will not because of what Jesus accomplished for us on the cross. Jesus' mission was to defeat all temptation; that is not our mission. While we encounter temptation, it is our purpose to implement the victory over temptation that Jesus gained for us. We don't have to duplicate Jesus' work, but to accomplish the purposes of Father for our life (Ephesians 2:10).

In his interaction with Jesus we see the shrewdness of Satan. He used Jesus' physical weakness and legitimate needs to tempt him to meet his own needs rather than trusting the Holy Spirit to care for him. This is the root of all temptation. Satan will try to tempt us to meet our own needs rather than trust Father to meet our needs. He will seek to convince us that, because God has not already met our needs, He won't ever meet our needs, and we therefore have to take matters into our own hands. Jesus had already fasted for 40 days, so Satan appeared to have a powerful argument that Father had forgotten him. However, Jesus refused to take the bait.

When the physical need failed to overcome Jesus, Satan used another shrewd tactic. Using Scripture to back up his temptation, he tempted Jesus to prove Jesus' own identity. Jesus' response shows not only the importance of knowing Scripture, but also knowing the heart of Father. Jesus knew the Father's heart so that there was no need for him to prove who he was. He also knew that it would hurt Father's heart if he felt it necessary to prove who he was. Like Jesus, we are Father's children; we have no need to prove who we are before men.

Finally, Satan tempted Jesus with a seemingly painless means to accomplish his purpose. He offered Jesus what appeared to be a good deal. Jesus had come to re-establish the Kingdom of God on earth. Satan offered all the kingdoms to Jesus if Jesus would worship him. While on the surface, it might appear attractive to us to cut corners in order to accomplish our purposes, Jesus kept the larger purpose in mind. The larger purpose is always worship, and God alone is to be worshiped, even if it requires a higher price.

Paul taught the Corinthians to be wise in the way that they live so that Satan might not use lack of wisdom as a means of temptation. Paul addressed the Corinthians' practice of married couples abstaining from sexual relations. While Paul did not tell them to stop this practice, he did give them guidelines. Abstinence should be practiced only when the husband and wife are in agreement, and for a specific time so that both parties may devote themselves to prayer (1 Corinthians 7:1-5). If either the husband or the wife insisted on abstinence without the consent from their spouse, they opened the possibility for Satan to tempt the party who had not agreed to practice abstinence. This wisdom should be kept in mind whenever we deny ourselves of something that also impacts others. While we may be strong enough to avoid temptation, those impacted may not be as strong, and our denial puts them at risk.

Satan will also use life difficulties in order to tempt one to shrink back from living in faith. He will use fear to hinder us from stepping out in boldness. Even though Paul had warned the Thessalonians about afflictions in connection with following Jesus, he still was concerned enough to send Timothy to make sure they were progressing in their faith (1 Thessalonians 3:5). It is a paradox, because even though we know that afflictions are associated with following Jesus, we still doubt the goodness of God when we encounter them. Jesus reminded his disciples that in this world, we will encounter tribulation (pressure), but to take courage because he has overcome the world (John 16:33). This is what seems to have concerned Paul regarding the Thessalonians.

Jesus warned the believers in Smyrna of this same tactic. In advance, Jesus told them that Satan would have some of them imprisoned for a short period (ten days) which would serve as a test (temptation). However, Jesus encouraged them to remain faithful. Having completed their test, they would receive the crown of life. Jesus told them specifically not to be afraid because they were to encounter suffering (Revelation 2:10).

Satan may use suffering as temptation to believe the lie that our Father does not care about us. As we remain faithful to Jesus, we discover that Father has not abandoned us, but gives us His presence in ways we would never have imagined possible. As we walk with Jesus, we discover that difficulty is actually an opportunity to encounter Jesus in ways previously unknown. Paul referred to this as the fellowship of suffering with Jesus (Philippians 3:10). As we persevere through tribulation with the strength of the Holy Spirit, Jesus reveals to us his great love that enabled him to endure suffering. In this experience, we draw closer to Jesus, which is the greatest gift that we can receive.

After Satan finished tempting Jesus in the wilderness, he withdrew, but not forever. He withdrew in order to renew his attack at a more opportune time (Luke 4:13). As we draw close to God, God will draw close to us, and Satan will flee (James 4:7-8). However, when Satan flees, we should not assume that he will not try again. He tried again with Jesus. For example, Satan used Jesus' close friend and disciple, Peter, as a spokesman for his evil agenda (Matthew 16:23). Satan did not abandon temptation; he merely looked for another opportunity. That means we must remain vigilant and pay attention to what is going on around us.

Trials as tests

As with many aspects of the Kingdom of God, temptations can have a counter-intuitive benefit. At times in the New Testament, the word "temptation," is not translated as such, but as "trial" or as we have already seen "test." In this case, a hardship or difficulty in life can also be a type of temptation to overcome. Trials and difficulties tempt us to give up and quit. Jesus overcame not only direct temptations by Satan, but also life difficulties that increased his discomfort in order to fulfill the Father's purpose for his life. Jesus encouraged his disciples when he told them that those who shared trials with him would receive authority in the kingdom of God (Luke 22:28-30). Jesus' words could be taken to mean not only the trials they shared when Jesus was alive upon the earth, but the trials that his disciples endured because they chose to follow Jesus after his ascension.

Paul alluded to the same concept when he gave his farewell speech to the Ephesian elders. While in Ephesus, Paul endured trials (temptations) at the hands of the Jews. The only reason that Paul had to endure these difficulties was because of his commitment to proclaim the gospel of Jesus to the Gentiles, which offended the Jews (Acts 20:19-21). The hardships that Paul faced could also be seen as temptations to give up in his proclamation of the gospel, but Paul declared that even though he faced such difficulties, he did not shrink back and return to the Pharisaical Judaism of his youth. He did not allow the trials to hinder his purpose on earth.

In contrast to Paul, the Galatians got sidetracked from the Gospel. However, Paul commended them for initially receiving him and his message with glad hearts though his condition was a trial to them (Galatians 4:14). It was not the trial that sidetracked them, but the false teaching which the Jews brought to them when they came after Paul's departure. The author of Hebrews encouraged the Jewish Christians of his day not succumb to their trials and warned them to not harden their hearts as they endured trials. He reminded them of the failure of the Jews in the desert who hardened their hearts at the time of trial (Hebrews 3:8; Psalm 95:7).

Our Request To God

One of the most surprising biblical statements about trials (temptations) is found in James when he taught believers to consider trials pure joy. Normally, we do not consider temptations or trials to be a reason for rejoicing, but James explained that through such circumstances, we develop endurance. Trials then function as a form of spiritual conditioning. As resistance causes our muscles to gain strength, likewise, trials in life causes our faith and spirit to grow stronger (James 1:2). James went on to explain that not only do we receive the benefit of endurance in this life, but we also receive recognition in the life to come. James referred to the crown of life received by all those who persevere under trials (James 1:12). Furthermore, James' teaching helps us grasp that trials are not random life occurrences. They have a purpose in our life. While Father is not the author of our trials, He allows what takes place to produce His purpose in our life. If Father's intended purpose has already been accomplished, then there is no longer need for further trial.

It is commonly understood that it is not only the most talented people who succeed, but those who refuse to give up when they face difficulty. Those who are talented may grow accustomed to things coming easily for them, but those who don't have the same level of talent learn to work harder without giving up; these are the ones who often succeed. These are the rags to riches stories that inspire the rest of us. James applied this well-known concept to our spiritual life.

Peter described a similar principle as James, focusing more on the finish line, rather than on the current benefits of enduring trials. What James referred to as the crown of life, Peter called an imperishable and undefiled inheritance reserved for those who overcome various trials in this life (1 Peter 1:4-6). It is the hope of a better future that empowers the follower of Jesus to persevere through the difficulties encountered because of his association with Jesus. Not only are we encouraged to persevere, but Peter went on to declare that we should not even be surprised when trials present themselves. In other words, we should expect trials because of our relationship with Jesus (1 Peter 4:12). Peter referred to our current situation as a fiery ordeal. Those who have gone to war have an expectation of being shot at. They train and prepare themselves for that eventuality. In the same way, since a follower of Jesus has chosen to live contrary to the world's majority, he or she should expect to encounter resistance and trials due to his or her decision.

Once again, in our battle against trials, we are not alone. While we have the fellowship of others who are on the same journey, Jesus also provides assistance and will rescue his own from overwhelming trials (2 Peter 2:9). He may reveal a way to move beyond the temptation and overcome it (1 Corinthians 10:13).

Jesus also said that sometimes the difficulty is limited in time so that his followers can persevere and not be overwhelmed (Matthew 24:22). Jesus notified his disciples that during a time of tribulation more intense than anything previously known, the days of trial would be cut short for their sake. At other times, Jesus promised his followers that because of their history of perseverance, he would protect them from certain trials that others would have to endure (Revelation 3:10). These promises give us confidence to know that, while we face trials of endurance, we will not be overwhelmed, because Jesus will not give to us more than we can bear.

Another source of encouragement to us are the prophets, who endured great trial and testing, yet remained faithful. They did so without seeing Jesus and receiving the encouragement of knowing their Savior would die for them and then defeat death by rising from the dead. Even with their limited knowledge, the prophets endured their trials. Isaiah died before he saw the fulfillment of the Messiah. Jeremiah died while the Israelites languished in captivity and before they would return to Jerusalem under Cyrus. Daniel likely died in Babylon, never returning to the land of his youth. Therefore, we with more information have all the more reason and resources to endure our trials (Hebrews 11:37).

When encouraged to throw himself off the precipice of the temple, Jesus reminded Satan that we are not to tempt God. While we endure trials, Paul instructed the Corinthians too that it is not our place to try or test God. In other words, we are not to force God's hand so that we require Him to prove His love and provision for us. He is already faithful to us, and we are not to continually test him (1 Corinthians 10:9; Matthew 4:7; Deuteronomy 6:16).

Wealth as temptation and a test

For those of us who live in the developed world, we have the added challenge of dealing with our affluence. It is important for us to recognize the dangerous snare the so-called American Dream lays out for us. While the American Dream promises comfort and an appearance of security, it has a high cost of superficiality and complacency. Jesus warned his disciples that we cannot serve two masters, God and money, because we love one and hate the other (Matthew 6:24). Paul was even more pointed in his warning, declaring that those who desire to get rich, which is at the core of the American Dream, will fall into temptation and lead them toward destruction. Paul even declared that some leave their faith in Jesus because they become so enamored with the attraction of riches (1 Timothy 6:9-10).

With this in mind, it is not surprising when we read Jesus' teaching to the disciples that it is easier for a camel to pass through the eye of a needle than for a rich man to enter into the Kingdom of Heaven (Luke 18:24-25). To the disciples, Jesus' words meant that no one could enter, but Jesus gave hope. With men it is surely impossible, but with God all things are possible (Luke 18:27). Chapter 19 of Luke demonstrates this very fact. A wealthy tax collector, Zacchaeus, gave away his wealth to the poor and restored what he had stolen, plus interest. Zacchaeus was a very wealthy man who entered the kingdom, not by the power of man, but by Father's transforming love revealed to him in Jesus.

In his Sermon on the Mount, Jesus indicated why it is so difficult for the wealthy to enter into the Kingdom. Jesus declared blessed those who are poor, hungry, sorrowful, and ostracized, but he declared woe upon those who are wealthy, well-fed, happy, and well spoken of by all (Luke 6:20-26). Those who he referred to as blessed have a constant motivation to do what Jesus said. They ask, seek and knock because they have need to seek out God, but those who have the woes of worldly blessings have no such need and therefore live in complacency (Luke 11:9-13). In other words, those who seek and achieve the American Dream may live in comfort and apparent security, but because of their affluence, they think that they have no need for God and do not seek Him out. According to Jesus, this is a woeful state in which to live.

Challenges as a temptation

At times, we are tempted to demonstrate what is already known to be true. In these situations, our sinful need to be recognized is touched. A number of times, Jesus was tempted to prove something about who he was. The people refused to recognize Jesus' claims and works. The Pharisees and the Jews repeatedly asked him to do a sign from Heaven to prove that he was from God. Rather than succumbing to their desire, Jesus rebuked them for being evil and asking for a sign (Matthew 16:1; Mark 8:11; Luke 11:16). In this case, Jesus turned temptation into an opportunity to correct a wrong attitude. With his example, Jesus showed us not only how to overcome temptation, but to use it as an opportunity to promote the Kingdom.

Others tested Jesus with questions designed to open up an opportunity to accuse him. Their question regarding the legality of divorce was one such occasion. Jesus directed them to God's created purpose for marriage and reminded them that it was hardness of heart that brought about divorce (Matthew 19:3; Mark 10:2). When the Jews tested Jesus regarding the payment of taxes, he revealed their sinful desire to test him. He knew that their question was not motivated by a desire to understand, but to find an opportunity to either criticize Jesus before the Jews, or condemn him before the Romans (Matthew 22:18; Mark 12:15; Luke 20:23). He avoided their dilemma, by revealing that man had responsibility both to God and to governing authorities. At other times some tested Jesus' response against what they knew Scripture to teach. They asked him to state the greatest commandment (Matthew 22:35). They brought a woman caught in adultery to see what he would do (John 8:6). On each occasion, Jesus responded wisely and gave them no further grounds to accuse him.

At times, we are internally tested because of our own desires that are not in line with what the Holy Spirit wants. These desires may even be legitimate desires but expressed at the wrong time (James 1:14).

Examples of tests

As already shown, the Greek word for, "tempt," has a variety of meanings. Consider the English word, "trunk." What does it mean? It can refer to an elephant's nose. It can refer to a type of box in which we ship things. It also refers to the rear portion of an automobile. In each case, the word refers to something that is a container. As we have seen the Greek word, translated most often "tempt," but also "test," has a foundational meaning of "to examine." Satan "examines" in order to produce failure and condemnation. However, twice in the New Testament the word refers to something from Jesus or Father. Of course, in this case, it would be inappropriate to translate it as "tempt," because this is foreign to Father's nature; He does, however test us from time to time to reveal to us what is in our heart and then to approve us when we pass the test.

For example, Jesus asked Philip how to feed the people gathered to hear his teaching. We read that Jesus said this to "test" Philip and see how he would respond (John 6:6). It appears that Jesus wanted to examine Philip's level of trust in Jesus' power. Would Philip grasp the concept that Jesus was able to address situations that, to Philip and the other disciples, appeared impossible? In Hebrews chapter eleven, the author used the same word for "test" to refer to Abraham's sacrifice of Isaac (Hebrews 11:17). After Abraham proved willing to sacrifice Isaac, God said to him that he knew that Abraham feared Him, because he did not withhold Isaac from Him (Genesis 22:12).

We also see the Greek word,, "periazo," used in different senses. It was translated as "attempt" when Paul and Silas' attempted to enter Bithynia (Acts 16:7). Later, Paul was accused of "attempting" to desecrate the temple (Acts 24:6). In these cases, the word "attempt" refers to an action done with the intent of success, but ultimately proved unsuccessful. At other times, "periazo" can refer to a self-examination. Paul instructed the believers of Corinth to "examine" meaning to "test" themselves and confirm their relationship with Jesus (2 Corinthians 13:5). Christians today may engage in the positive activity of testing. Jesus praised the church in Ephesus because they "tested" those who claimed to be apostles (Revelation 2:2). Their activity reminds us of the praise that the Bereans received because they searched the Scriptures to make sure what Paul taught was consistent with Scripture (Acts 17:11).

Nevertheless, most occurrences of this word refer to a temptation toward sin. Peter rebuked Ananias for his action which tested the Holy Spirit (Acts 5:9). Later, Peter taught the church that they should not test God by requiring the Gentiles to live in a way that God did not require of them (Acts 15:10). The author of Hebrews warned believers that they should not act like their forefathers in the desert who tested God with their continual complaining (Hebrews 3:9).

James clearly reveals the difference in meaning of the word. He instructed the believers that when they are "tempted," they should not claim that God is "tempting" them, because God is not "tempted," nor can he "tempt" (James 1:13). James does not contradict the use of the word found in John and Hebrews. While John used "periazo" to refer to Jesus' examination of Philip regarding feeding the crowd and the author of Hebrews used it in reference to God's command for Abraham to sacrifice Isaac, James used the word in James 1:13 to affirm that God is never tempted to sin, nor does he ever tempt anyone to sin. Therefore as we appeal to Father not to lead us into sin, we can be sure that he will respond.

Summary

Of all the declaration prayers in the Lord's Prayer, only one is negative. "Do not lead us into temptation." Because it is a negative command, it has a different grammatical form than all the others. If Matthew had maintained the same form, the meaning would have been something that was false. Rather than a request of God not to lead us into temptation, the meaning would have been, "stop leading us into temptation." To avoid presenting a false view of the nature of God, Matthew changed grammatical forms, making this prayer unique. We have seen that the Greek word "periazo" can take on various meanings, even positive ones, depending upon the context. For example at times the word is used of God's testing the faith of man, as in the case of Abraham. However, when the word is used of man testing God or Jesus, the action is clearly wrong. When God brings a test, the purpose is always good. But when Satan or man brings temptation, the intent is to reveal fault. The intent of the test or trial reveals whether the action is good or evil. In a few instances the word can have a neutral meaning to indicate an action taken. In those cases it is translated as "attempt."

Temptation can impact us in various forms. Satan may use our legitimate human needs as means to tempt us to ignore God's provision and leading in our lives. At other times, men seeking their own purposes may tempt us to prove ourselves so that we will be viewed higher in their eyes. Jesus clearly revealed that this action was to be avoided. Good things like wealth may also become an occasion for temptation because they may distract us from our highest calling to love God. In these cases, wealth becomes like an idol even if it was originally given as a blessing.

Our request to Father signifies our constant, dependent relationship with him. He is the one to whom we run when we are in need of help. Our prayer that we not be led into temptation is an indication of our need for Father's help.

Questions for Reflection

1. Reflect on those situations which cause you to experience temptation. In what ways does Father offer you a way out of temptation (1 Corinthians 10:13)?

Our Request To God

2. How has overcoming temptation developed strength in your life?

Papa, I recognize my need for your strength and protection. I ask you to protect me from those challenges in life for which I am yet unprepared. I ask for the wisdom to recognize when I am being tempted. Give me patience to reject the apparent benefit of succumbing to the temptation and to wait for that which is received from your hand. Amen.

Chapter 9
Our Call To Father For Deliverance
Matthew 6:13

The Christian is one who places all of his hopes and future in Jesus. He learns not to place his hopes in the things of this world: job, relationships, wealth, and skills. Like David, he learns to seek his refuge from Jesus. As a child looks to his parents to meet his needs for food, shelter, clothing, and security, so also the Christian learns to depend on the provision of Jesus. Look at the world and see that we are in a war with evil. As I write this chapter two tragedies have recently struck. In Portland, Oregon a young gunman killed two people in a shopping mall filled with Christmas shoppers. A few days later another gunman killed twenty-seven people, twenty of whom were children ages five through seven. The stories seem to be strangely similar. Two young men in their early twenties, both of whom were considered nice and polite by friends. With these tragedies, people naturally ask why and what can we do? Others raise the issue of gun control, assuming that if guns are taken away from people, the danger is reduced. However, gun control cannot resolve the violence in hearts. Schools across the country send out communication assuring parents that they have adequate security in their school and tips on how to counsel their children. However the question remains, can anyone deliver us from the evil that even creeps into suburban shopping malls and quiet elementary schools which are located in affluent neighborhoods and believed to be safe? If we can't be safe in suburban shopping malls and elementary schools, then where can we be safe? More regulations, more police, and more security may limit the violence, but it always seems to morph into new and more creative expressions, causing continued destruction in the lives of its victims. The problem is that evil resides in places that laws and regulatory agencies cannot touch. It resides in the human heart, which only the Spirit of God can touch and bring healing. Jesus' final prayer command touches the issue of evil in the human heart. It is a recognition that only the Spirit of God can protect us from evil that has invaded every area of human existence, the community, schools, and even the nuclear family.

The last petition in the Lord's Prayer is the other side of the coin to our request of not being led into temptation. Jesus taught us not only to desire the avoidance of temptation, but to be delivered from evil. Much of following Jesus is a partnership between us and the Holy Spirit. As we overcome temptation and the trials of our life, the Holy Spirit protects us from evil. If temptation cannot get to us, then evil is limited in our life. With God's power, we defeat temptation; then evil is defeated before it can get any closer to us. On the contrary, if we are not seeking to overcome temptation, we are inviting evil to rule us. While defeating temptation can limit evil's impact in our life, it does not remove evil from us altogether, which is why we must declare to Father to deliver us from it. In this chapter, we will look at what the New Testament teaches about our being delivered from evil.

Deliver

As we've seen, we live in a world attacked by evil. We encounter it every day of our life. At times we recognize the battle, at other times we are oblivious to its presence because we are not sensitive enough to it or have become desensitized to it. Since we face evil consistently, we have a great need to be delivered from it and its effects. At times, we get a glimpse of Father's power to protect us from evil. For example, we narrowly miss being in an auto accident. Seemingly out of the blue, a thought comes to mind that later we realize led us to make a decision that protected us from disaster. One afternoon, I was riding my bicycle down a steep hill, picking up speed along the way. About half-way down the hill, the thought came to me to slow down. Typically, I never slowed riding down that hill; actually I tried to go as fast as I could, but this day I slowed down. Seconds later, my rear wheel unexpectedly locked up. Since I had slowed down I was able to control the situation without falling, but if I hadn't slowed down, I easily could have had an accident. I do not believe this "apparently random" thought was a coincidence, but an example of my loving, heavenly Father delivering me from evil. An unexpected delay causes us to leave for an appointment later than we had planned, but on the way we pass an accident that had just occurred. If we had left on time, would it have been us involved in the accident? Have you ever considered that random, "coincidental" incidents which delay you, might actually protect you from evil? We will never know, but Father does. We know that Father protects His children from evil.

The Bible indicates that our being delivered from evil is impacted by prayer. Here, in the Lord's Prayer, the final request is to be delivered from evil (Matthew 6:13; Luke 11:4). Jesus' teaching that we issue a declaration to the Father to deliver us from evil implies that it has an important role in our being delivered. As we've seen earlier, Scripture teaches that the prayer of a righteous man is powerful and effective (James 5:16).

Jesus' command to the disciples in the Garden to watch and pray so that they would not fall into temptation is applicable. Jesus knew that there was danger not only for him, but also for his followers. He had earlier warned Peter that Satan had asked to sift Peter as wheat, but Jesus had prayed that his faith would not fail. The implication is that if Jesus had failed to pray, Peter's faith may have failed. Jesus also warned Peter that he would deny him three times that very night. Later that evening, Jesus urged Peter to pray, but Peter failed to heed Jesus' warning. Jesus' warnings to the disciples indicate that they should have prayed to be delivered from evil. It is implied that if he had prayed, Peter would not have succumbed to evil and denied Jesus. His faith was not what failed; however he failed to pray to be delivered from evil and therefore denied Jesus. In other

143

words, our praying to be delivered from evil has real implications for our lives.

As we issue this declaration to Father, we acknowledge a couple of things. First, we acknowledge the truth that evil exists and can impact us. Second, we do need to be delivered from evil and cannot accomplish that feat on our own. If we believed that we could conquer evil on our own, we would not ask to be delivered from it. Therefore, we are dependent upon Father to deliver us. In other words, every time that we declare our need to be delivered, we acknowledge our need for a Savior, which is a confirmation of who Jesus is. Our declaration affirms Jesus as Savior in the Kingdom of God. As we experience Jesus' power and protection, we are fulfilling the first declarations of the Lord's prayer, "hallowed be Your Name," and, "Your Kingdom come and Your Will be done on earth as it is in Heaven." Our protected life reveals that Father is Holy and fulfills His promises to protect us. His power to protect us reveals that His Kingdom is being established upon the earth. When Jesus is affirmed as Savior, then Father's heavenly will is being accomplished on earth through our prayer.

As we've seen in Jesus as Savior, the concept of "save" and "deliver" are, at times linked in the New Testament. Paul declared that some day all of Israel will be saved, because the Deliverer (Jesus) will come from Zion (Romans 11:26). Paul made this point by quoting the prophet Isaiah (Isaiah 59:20). In this way, Paul linked the biblical concepts of deliverance and salvation. At times, the Greek verb "sozo" most often translated as "save" also means "deliver." The individual whom Jesus delivered from a legion of demons was declared to "be well" or "saved" (Luke 8:36). As Jesus delivered the demonic from evil, he was also causing the Kingdom of Heaven to come and function on the earth. As a part of our salvation from sin, Father removes us from one kingdom and brings us into another. This process of moving from one "evil" or "dark" kingdom to the

Our Call To Father For Deliverance

Kingdom of Heaven is another example of our deliverance from evil (Colossians 1:13). We call this process "salvation," or "conversion," which is a past event, but we live out the implications of that event.

Our moving from one kingdom to another engages us in a conflict that we have not experienced before. For this reason, Paul instructed the Ephesian believers to put on their "spiritual armor." In that lesson, Paul revealed to the Ephesians that, contrary to what we might think, our battle is not against people, but against spiritual powers active in the world and heavenly places (Ephesians 6:12). Paul identified for them several pieces of our armor: truth, righteousness, the Gospel of peace, faith, our salvation, and the word of God (Ephesians 6:13-17). For many years, I assumed that Paul's reference to the "word of God" referred to Scripture. Recently, I studied the phrase "word of God." I discovered that most of the time the phrase referred to the spoken word of truth, not Scripture. Earlier, we saw how important it was to declare Father's name Holy, to declare His Kingdom and the fulfillment of His Will. In our war against evil, one of our weapons is a spoken declaration of Father's Word. Through His gifts of spiritual armor, Father has given to us a means to be delivered from evil. Again, we see how we labor along with Father to defeat evil in our life and participate in our own deliverance.

Evil comes in many forms. As we've seen, it is at times addressed generically as evil. At other times, evil is descriptive of something or someone else. Men of the world give themselves over to evil and in so doing, become enemies of the kingdom. Zechariah, the father of John the Baptist, prophesied after the birth of his son, that through the coming of the Messiah whom his son would announce, Israel would be delivered from its enemies (Luke 1:74-76). Strong and faithful as he was, Paul acknowledged his own need for prayer in order to be rescued from evil men (2 Thessalonians 3:1-2). When Paul wrote both letters to the Thessalonians, he was being chased down by Jews who hated the Gospel. The only reason for which Paul suffered was because he had declared the Gospel to the Thessalonians. The Jews chased him out of town, then followed him to Berea, from which he traveled to Athens (Acts 17:5-15). Later, Paul acknowledged that his enemies had not diminished in their efforts against him.

As he traveled toward Jerusalem, Paul reminded the Romans that he was in need of their prayers so that he would be delivered from unbelieving Jews in Jerusalem (Romans 15:31). Luke's description of Paul's trip to Jerusalem confirms Paul's concern and need of prayer. Lies had been spread in Jerusalem about Paul so that even a riot erupted when Paul entered the temple. Although Paul was arrested, because of the intervention of the Romans, he was not killed by the irate Jews (Acts 21:27-36). At the end of his life, just prior to his being martyred for his testimony for Jesus, Paul reminded Timothy of Father's faithfulness in rescuing him from the evil men who followed him through Asia Minor. He went on to remind Timothy that every person who desires to follow Jesus will experience persecution (2 Timothy 3:11-12). Paul's words to Timothy encourage us to follow Jesus' instruction to pray for our deliverance from evil. Later again to Timothy, Paul informed him of what happened during the first phase of his trial before the Emperor Nero. Although he was alone, Jesus stood with Paul strengthening him to the point that he could boldly proclaim the Gospel in the court of the emperor. Although Paul recognized his life was about to end, he knew that even in death, he would be rescued and brought into the heavenly Kingdom of Jesus (2 Timothy 4:17-18). Because of Jesus' victory over death, he has defeated death's vile hold over us. Paul lived free because he knew he had been and was continuing to be delivered from evil.

The greatest and last evil that Jesus defeated was death (1 Corinthians 15:54-55). From death, all men need a Savior, so

Our Call To Father For Deliverance

that Paul called out in his letter to the Romans seeking the one who would deliver him from the evil of death associated with his earthly body (Romans 7:24). The answer to his own question is Jesus. So that even as we live in a body of flesh that is passing away, we have hope in Jesus. Even though followers of Jesus still must endure death, it not the end. As Paul reminded the Corinthians, death no longer carries the same sting. Because of Jesus' victory, his followers do not grieve as those of the world do. Without Jesus, there is no hope for those who have lost loved ones; they are gone forever, but in Jesus, death no longer holds a threat (1 Thessalonians 4:13-14). Since death is defeated, Paul could actually view his own death positively (Philippians 1:23-24). When Paul cried out with the question of who would deliver him from the body of death, he was looking to Jesus (Romans 7:24).

From Paul's letter he faced life-threatening situations while in Asia (modern Asia Minor), but none of those dangerous situations took his life. Paul understood the power of Jesus to keep the evil of death from overtaking him (2 Corinthians 1:10-11). As Jesus taught his disciples to declare that God deliver them from evil, Paul experienced the fulfillment of that prayer multiple times in Asia and believed that Jesus would continue to protect him through his own prayers and those of the Corinthians. Paul realized that it was not his own efforts, plans or strategies that preserved his life, but his and the believers' prayers to that end. Literally, Father delivered him from evil.

Furthermore, there seems to be a transition in Paul's life and ministry. Prior to Paul's arrival in Corinth, he was consistently forced to flee for his life: from Damascus, Jerusalem, Thessalonica and Beria. In Corinth, Jesus appeared to Paul, telling him not to be afraid or be silent. Jesus' command to Paul not to be afraid implied that he was at that time afraid and also silent (Acts 18:9-10). Jesus revealed two things to Paul. Jesus had many followers in Corinth and he would be with Paul. From

147

Our Call To Father For Deliverance

that point, Paul never fled from any city. In fact, when believers urged him not to continue his journey to Jerusalem, Paul continued anyway, because he trusted the leading and protection of the Spirit. From Corinth onwards, Paul's life was marked by an increase in courage in the face of life-threatening danger.

Another apostle familiar with the rigors of battling evil was Peter. He encouraged his readers by reminding them of how Father preserved Noah through a global flood, while the rest of the world perished. Father again preserved righteous Lot amidst the wicked citizens of Sodom. Since Father had faithfully preserved his righteous followers in the past, He surely would do the same for those who love Jesus (2 Peter 2:5-9). Father will not only rescue Jesus' followers from evil, but also from temptation.

Not only is Father near to us when we face evil situations, but He is near those who are brokenhearted (Psalm 34:18 and 147:3). Those who face tragedy in their lives, Papa draws near in unique ways. That nearness can keep us from evil and serves to deliver us from bitterness. Several years ago, I was present when a friend went to be with Jesus after fighting cancer for a number of years. There was an amazing sense of the Holy Spirit's presence in the hospital room as he slipped from this world into eternity. The nurse testified to the powerful sense of peace when a follower of Jesus passes from this world. Even in a very difficult and painful time, there is a peace that settles in. Papa extends His supernatural presence and grace to those who face tragedy and draws near to them with comfort.

As a glimpse of what will happen for all those who follow Jesus, Father raised Jesus from the dead. Like we will someday, Jesus endured death, but death could not contain him. Because the same victory over death has been given to all those who follow Jesus, death holds no lasting power over any believer (1 Thessalonians 1:10). Right now, we wait for Jesus to come back; Scripture teaches that, at that time there will be judgment for sin, but those who know Jesus will be saved from the future judgment and wrath, because Jesus already endured it for them.

Jesus delivered

When Jesus was crucified, numerous ironies were at work. The people scoffed and ridiculed him, challenging him to descend from the cross if he was God's son. They believed that if he were God's son, he would surely be delivered from the cross, because anyone who is hung on a tree is cursed. However, they failed to understand the heart of Father and the magnitude of their own sin. Jesus hung on the cross because he was God's son (Matthew 27:43). The people failed to recognize both that they needed a Savior from the judgment to come and that Jesus was the Savior who was dying in their place.

Summary

The fact that Jesus taught us to pray for deliverance results in a number of implications. First, anyone who asks for deliverance recognizes his own need. If you don't have any needs, you don't need deliverance. Asking for deliverance implies that we recognize Father as a Savior who is our deliverer. We only appeal for deliverance from those whom we believe have the power and willingness to do so. If we didn't believe that Father had the power and willingness to save us, it would be foolish for us to ask him for deliverance. Ultimately, Scripture teaches that we need to be delivered from the power of sin, death, and their impact upon our life. Once delivered, the fear of death is removed for us and for our loved ones who follow Jesus.

However, evil has a broader impact in the world than death. It impacts all areas of life, including both relationships and circumstances. Although followers of Jesus will encounter evil

Our Call To Father For Deliverance

men and endure evil situations, they have the power through Jesus to overcome them (Romans 8:37). The point is that we have a deliverer who frees us to live according to our deliverance.

Questions for Reflection

1. Praying to be delivered offers real protection from evil. How does this truth impact the way your pray?

2. Why do you think men like Peter failed to pray when warned of a dangerous future situation?

3. How does the world seek to convince us not to pray for deliverance from evil?

Papa, I thank you for delivering me from evil. I recognize your power and authority over the rulers, powers, world forces, and spiritual forces of wickedness in the world. With your power and protection, I have no need to fear or feel anxious, because you are a shield all around me. May my understanding of your deliverance grow. Remind me to continue to ask for your protection from evil in my life. Amen.

Chapter 10
Jesus Reveals Results Of The Kingdom
Matthew 6:13

One of the questions I've always dealt with in my relationship with Jesus has been how to live in the world and not be of it. How do I live in the world, care about people in the world as Jesus did, yet not be distracted by what is in the world? Over the last year as I've looked at the Lord's Prayer, it has occurred to me that it is a summary of how to live in the world and not of the world. We derive our identity from our heavenly Father. "Our Father who is in Heaven, hallowed be Your name," the name we've received from Father. "Your Kingdom come," the same Kingdom that is ours as Father's children. "Your will be done on earth as it is in Heaven" reveals the reason we are on earth. Just like Jesus, we desire that Father's purposes be accomplished over our own comfort.

We receive all of our physical and spiritual provision from our heavenly Father. We seek our daily bread; Jesus is the bread of life. We love and forgive, because Father has first loved and forgiven us. Our physical needs are promised to us as we seek the Kingdom and as we seek our daily spiritual provision from Jesus. Our forgiveness of others, reveals that we are children of God. In a way, the Lord's prayer is an explanation of how we seek first the Kingdom and its righteousness, and all these things (our material needs) will be added to us. As we follow Father and draw near to him, then we overcome temptation; evil is defeated in our lives, primarily because our affections are directed toward our Father in heaven, which removes the footholds Satan may have from which to tempt us. Satan can only effectively tempt us in areas where we have either needs or affections. Satan sought to tempt Jesus in areas of his physical and emotional needs. However, Jesus' affections were stronger for the Father and the Kingdom than they were for things of this world. Therefore, Satan failed in his attempts to tempt Jesus away from his relationship with Father.

Jesus Reveals The Results Of The Kingdom

Our identity as children of the Father and our mission to defeat evil, reveal what the New Testament declares, that we are at war. The picture of Joshua and the children of Israel taking the promised land is a picture of our life now as we expand the Kingdom of God all over the earth. However, we don't do it in the same manner as Joshua, because our battle is not against flesh and blood, but against the powers and principalities of this world.

The last half of Matthew 6:13, "Yours is the Kingdom and the power and the glory forever," is a final declaration. Unlike the previous statements, it is neither a command nor an expression of a desire, but an affirmation of fact. Before we look at what is communicated in this statement, it is important to address an important question. If you use a King James Version, the statement is written in the same format as the previous statements. However, if you read a New American Standard Version, this last part is in brackets. The English Standard Version and the New International Version leave it out all together and place it in a footnote. The question is, why is this sentence treated differently?

The answer to this question relates to the question of how we received the Bible, particularly the New Testament. While we have evidence that the entire New Testament was written in the first century, we do not have any of the original manuscripts. We don't have the original manuscripts that Paul or any of the Gospel writers penned. Over the centuries, the New Testament was copied by hand. As copies were transported to new areas and replicated, variations occurred. It is important to understand that none of the variations change the meaning of the passage from which they are a found.

Scholars theorize that this might have happened if a note was made in a copy, somewhat like when we write a note in the margin of our Bibles. Years after the copy was made, the scribe copying that particular manuscript had to decide whether to include the note in the text. If the copyist chose to add that note to the text in his copy, a variation occurred. Today, we have thousands of complete or partial manuscripts of the New Testament that are part of what we call textual families. Some are the Byzantine texts from Asia Minor, Alexandrian texts from Egypt, Western Texts from Italy and Western Europe, and Caesarean texts from Palestine along with several others. Each of these areas have thousands of manuscripts and are identified by region. In the late 300's, Jerome translated the Scriptures from Greek into Latin. This Latin translation was called the Vulgate and became the official version of the Roman Catholic Church until Vatican II in the early 1960's. At that time, the Roman Catholic Church permitted Roman Catholic Versions of the Bible to be published in modern languages.

In the 1500's, the Roman Catholic Scholar Erasmus wanted to update the Vulgate and produce a Greek version of the New Testament. He gathered the best manuscripts that he had at the time. The Greek version that he developed has become known as the Received Text from which our King James Bible was translated in the late 1600's. In the 500 years since Erasmus, we've discovered more and older Greek manuscripts than Erasmus had at his disposal. The Modern translations like the New American Standard, the New International Version, the English Standard Version, and others, used those texts. For this reason some verses are footnoted or put in brackets to identify the fact that the verse, set of verses, or partial verse is not found in manuscripts considered older. The latter part of Matthew 6:13 is an example of one of these variations.

Before finalizing on which version is preferable, scholars use principles to help them determine whether they think a certain variation is more reliable than others. They do look at the age of the manuscript, but they also typically prefer a shorter, simpler version to a longer, more complicated one. Translators do this because of the human tendency to add an explanation and create a longer version. In other words, it is easier to explain how a copyist might have added a phrase, rather than how a phrase might have been left out. Since we do not have the original manuscripts, it is impossible for us to say with certainty that one variation is right and another wrong. Even if we were to leave out the second half of Matthew 6:13, the meaning of the Lord's Prayer remains the same. All that is contained in that phrase is confirmed in other parts of the New Testament. The Kingdom does belong to the Father, it is also characterized by power, glory, and eternity.

It is important for us to have a reason to explain variations in the Bible in response to some who say that the Bible is filled with errors and cannot be trusted. Having said all of that to explain the questions that may arise when you look at Matthew 6:13, let's take a look at it.

Power Definition

The Greek word "dynamis" often translated as "power" used in Matthew 6:13, is the Greek word from which we get the English words "dynamite" and "dynamic." However, in the New Testament, it is also one of the words that has been translated also as "miracle." Therefore, the word, "power," is linked to the supernatural expressions of power released as we live out the Kingdom. In the parable of the talents, the word is also translated as "abilities" (Matthew 25:15). The master gave to each of his servants according to each of their "ability" (dynamis). The word can also refer to Satan's power. Jesus conferred to his delegation the "authority" over the "power" of the enemy, so that nothing could hurt Jesus' followers (Luke 10:19). Even though Satan may have "power," the follower of Jesus has authority over demonic "power" in Jesus' name.

Jesus Reveals The Results Of The Kingdom

In 1 Corinthians 12, "dynamis" is used to describe one of the spiritual gifts, the working of "miracles" (dynamis). One of the gifts of the spirit is the ability to do supernatural works, as Jesus did, authenticating the power of the gospel, just like Jesus did (1 Corinthians 12:10, 28-29). In 1 Corinthians 12:10, the word is combined with "workers," the word from which we get our word, "energy." However, in 1 Corinthians 12:28-29, the word "miracle" (dynamis) is used by itself, but in English we have to supply the verb, "work," in order for it to make sense.

Spiritual gifts

Let me add here, that although we use the phrase, "spiritual gifts," the Greek word for "gift" is not used here. The Greek word for "gift" is used in reference to salvation and the spirit, as in "the gift of the Spirit" and "the gift of salvation." In 1 Corinthians 12:1, where we read "now concerning spiritual gifts," the word "gift" is supplied in English to make sense. The word is "spiritual," literally "spirituals," (Or as I like to translate "spiritual stuff"). Later in the chapter, Paul uses a different word, "charismati," from the Greek word, "xaris," or "grace." Of course this is where we get our English words, "charisma" and "charismatic." The word "gift" is still not present. Again I like to translate this as "grace stuff." So what we call, "spiritual gifts," are actually things of the Spirit and of grace. The "spiritual gifts" are the results of the Holy Spirit dwelling in us and releasing Father's grace in us.

Paul used the word "power" in an interesting context in 1 Corinthians 14:11. He said in reference to speaking in tongues, that when he could not understand the meaning (dynamis) of the word, it was as if he were listening to a barbarian language. The use of the word "dynamis" (power) translated as "meaning," gives a different understanding of Paul's words than we might think. We normally think of "meaning" as in terms of

Jesus Reveals The Results Of The Kingdom

"definition," but Paul affirmed that words have "power" when we understand them. In other words, Paul says that if he cannot understand the word, he can not be impacted by its power. Paul did not say this to dismiss the importance of tongues, but to explain their function and to underscore the importance of a prophetic word that is spoken in a way that is understood. Paul's use of the word, "power," implies that the spoken word has great impact when understood. Paul's use of "power" in 1 Corinthians 14:11, reminds us of James' instruction on the tongue in James 3:9-10. Our tongues (words) have the power to bless or curse. With them, we either build up or tear down. In James 5, we read the power of spoken prayer. Through prayer, Elijah stopped the rain for three and a half years, then he restored it with another prayer (James 5:16-18).

In 2 Corinthians 12, we have another unusual use of the word "dynamis.". Jesus revealed to Paul, that Jesus' strength (dynamis) was magnified in Paul's weakness. Jesus' revelation to Paul reminds us that when we are strong, then our tendency is to utilize our strength and resources to advance the Kingdom, but when we are weak and lack resources, then we become more dependent upon Jesus' power. The same contrast is made of Jesus in the following chapter. Paul wrote that Jesus was crucified in weakness, but raised in the power (dynamis) of the Father (2 Corinthians 13:4). The exact two words are used of Jesus, as they were of Paul in 2 Corinthians 12. Paul's two examples reveal a connection between our weakness and the release of God's power.

Power Revelations

In the New Testament, we also get glimpses of this power not only being defined, but also revealed. In Luke 9:1 and 10:19, we see that the power Jesus worked with is transferable to his followers. In Luke 9 the word is used in reference to his twelve disciples who healed the sick and cast out demons. In chapter 10 the word is used in reference to Satan's power, but the "authority" given to the seventy was even greater (Luke 10:19). In other words, the power received through the authority given by Jesus is greater than the power that Satan possesses.

In Romans 1:16, Paul revealed that the proclamation of the Gospel is a release of power to grant salvation to those who accept it. This is evidenced through people's lives being completely transformed by an encounter with Jesus. Twice in Romans 15, Paul spoke of the revelation of God's power. First in verse 13, through the power of the Holy Spirit, we abound in hope. In other words, our hope is not based on things of this world that are passing away, but on the power of the Holy Spirit that works in us. He follows up in verse 19, speaking of his focus on bringing the Gentiles to faith in Jesus, doing so through signs and wonders by the power of the Spirit.

Paul, in Romans 1:16, linked the word, "power," to salvation. We see the same combination in the account of the woman who suffered from bleeding. Believing that she would be healed if she touched Jesus' cloak, she touched the hem of it as he passed by. When she did so, Jesus felt "virtue"/"power" leave from him. The text says that she was instantly "made well". However, the Greek word "sozo" translated as "made well" is the verb often translated "to save" (Matthew 9:21-22; Mark 5:28, 34; Luke 8:44-48). The release of Jesus' power, resulted in the woman being saved (healed or delivered) from her disease.

In Luke's account of the woman's healing, Jesus previously had commanded the legion of demons to leave the man. Afterwards it was apparent to the the people that he had been "healed," or saved (Luke 8:36). In the account of casting out the legion of demons the word "power" was not used, but a few verses later in the following account, the word "power" does

Jesus Reveals The Results Of The Kingdom

occur in relation to the healing of the woman who was bleeding. The verbal proclamation of the Gospel of Jesus has the power to save. The proclamation also carries with it the power to heal physical infirmities and to deliver from the demonic realm. David prophesied of this power, when he declared in Psalm 103 that the Lord forgives all our sins and heals all of our diseases. Those two phrases are parallel, indicating that if one is true, then the other is true as well (Psalm 103:3).

The link between salvation and power reminds us that the Gospel is more than a message or information about Jesus; the Gospel *is* Jesus. Jesus said that he is the way, the truth and the life, no man comes to the Father except through him (John 14:6). Transformation comes through relationship. This is why the coming of the Spirit was so important. Jesus actually told the disciples it was better that he went away, because of the Spirit's coming (John 16:7). Earlier, he informed the disciples that any one who believed in Jesus would do greater works than Jesus did, implying the release of Jesus' power and authority in the life of any believer living and walking in the Spirit (John 14:12). Just prior to his ascension, Jesus commanded his disciples to remain in Jerusalem until they were clothed with power, again referring to the Spirit who would come a mere ten days later (Acts 1:6-8). As we walk in relationship with Jesus through communion with the Spirit, we will observe life transforming power released in ourselves and in the lives of others.

In Paul's final letter, which was written from a cold and dirty hole in the ground shortly before he was executed for his faith in Jesus, Paul declared to Timothy that Father has not given to us a Spirit of timidity, but one of love, power, and self-control. The power that sustained Paul in prison came from the Spirit. The result of that power is that no follower of Jesus should allow himself to be ashamed of the testimony of Jesus, his followers, or of the Gospel, for the Gospel is the "power" of God (2 Timothy 1:7-8).

Jesus Reveals The Results Of The Kingdom

The power of the Spirit enabled Paul on one hand, to do signs and wonders which brought the Gentiles to faith in Jesus; yet, on the other hand it supplied him with the joy and self-control to have hope in Jesus though in prison and knowing that he would soon be executed.

Definition of Glory

Sometimes it is hard to define kingdom concepts. For example, what is "glory?" At times it is identified with "light." In Luke 2:9, we read that the "glory" of the Lord shone around the angel who had announced Jesus' birth. In that case, the Lord's glory has the capacity to "shine." This was also the indication on the Mount of Transfiguration, when it says that Peter, James, and John saw the "glory" shine around Jesus (Luke 9:32). Years after encountering Jesus on the road to Damascus, Paul described the light that blinded him as the "glory;" some newer translations have "brightness" here, but the word is "glory" (Acts 22:11).

However, there are times when the "glory" of God is revealed, not with literal light, but with power to do miracles. After Jesus changed the water to wine, John wrote that the disciples observed God's glory in Jesus (John 2:11). There is no reference to light shining from the wine or Jesus at that time; nevertheless, his glory was present. Through Jesus' manifested "glory," his disciples believed in him. Later, before Jesus returned to Bethany to raise Lazarus, he told his disciples that Lazarus' death would result in the glory of God. When he told them to remove the stone and Martha objected, he reminded her that he had told her she would see the glory of God (John 11:4, 40). When Jesus called Lazarus from the tomb and he exited, there again was no indication of light; although, God's glory was revealed.

Jesus Reveals The Results Of The Kingdom

Even more amazing, the glory that was revealed in Jesus also dwells in us and will be revealed in us. Paul mentioned that the present struggles we have in this life cannot be compared to the glory that will be revealed to us (Romans 8:18). In other words, God's glory dwells in us, but it has not yet been revealed to its future extent. This follows because of who we are. Since we are the children of Father God, then it follows that we will reveal the same glory, the same glory that was revealed in Jesus. As we proclaim the Kingdom today, then we should expect to see Father's glory manifest as light, like the shepherds, the disciples and Paul did. At other times, his glory will be revealed through works of power (miracles, signs and wonders), because that is another way the glory manifested itself in the Bible.

Forever

One of the frustrating aspects of this world is the reality that things do not last. Although we say we own things, we really don't. At most, we have temporary control over things, but since we are here only temporarily, we cannot really say that we own anything, because everything we claim to own will be left behind when we go. After our departure, someone else, who will one day pass away as well, will take possession of it. Then, everything we temporarily have wears out while we use it. Our bodies and our possessions both wear out and require attention. You attend a memorial service and see pictures of the deceased in younger days and it is difficult to comprehend they are now gone. After my graduation, from college I purchased a brand new 1980 Datsun (Nissan) 310. I loved that car. That vehicle was so shiny and new, but after driving it eight years the clutch wore out and the seats were faded. Today, over thirty years later, it is likely sitting in a junk yard or is part of something else in the form of recycled materials. There is something that feels wrong about that, things wearing out and people dying. Solomon declared that God has placed eternity in the hearts of man, which explains why we struggle so much with the temporary and broken nature of our present world (Ecclesiastes 3:11). Inherently, we know that death is not how things are supposed to be.

In Matthew 6, Jesus warned us about investing in things that will not last (Matthew 6:19-21). We are to live for the Kingdom because it will never pass away. Paul revealed to us that everything in this world has been subjected to corruption due to man's rebellion against God; therefore, it will pass away (Romans 8:19-25). The fact that the Bible declares that due to man's sin, the world was corrupted, leads us to wonder what the world was like before the fall. Were the physical laws different before?

The Lord's Prayer ends, declaring that the Kingdom and power and glory will last forever. That means that the Kingdom is fundamentally different than the world. To last forever, it must run with different physical laws than the world that is passing away, wearing out, and running down. In the world, even though energy is neither lost nor gained, it does get transferred into non-reusable forms like heat. When I was twelve I received a new Schwinn 3 speed bicycle. My parents gave me a headlight that was powered by a small generator, which in turn was powered by the back wheel. I loved riding as fast as I could to see how bright the light would get. I asked my dad why we didn't put little generators on everything so that we could power the world. That was when I got my first lesson on the Laws of Thermodynamics. With the use of energy, it gets transformed into less usable forms. For example, my energy used to pedal my bicycle was transferred to light, heat from the light and friction in the generator. Not all my energy was transferred efficiently to light, but some was expended in heat and friction.

In nuclear fission, energy is released through the division of atoms, but in nuclear fusion, more energy is released than what

Jesus Reveals The Results Of The Kingdom

was needed to establish the reaction. That is why scientists hope to develop nuclear fusion to solve our energy problems. However, this may be a glimpse into kingdom physics. Like nuclear fusion when a multiplication of energy takes place, in the multiplication of the bread through Jesus' word, a little was multiplied leaving more in the end than the disciples began with. Might there be a release of power through unification?

The last time the world was unified was Babel (Genesis 11). However it was unified in opposition to God. That was when God confused man's language to prevent man from further progress against God's Kingdom. However in Acts 2, we see the beginning of a return to a unified language. Although many people spoke different languages that day, they each understood the language that the believers were speaking. Acts 2 is a reflection of Kingdom unity and a restoration of the division that took place in Genesis 11. In Revelation we read that the Kingdom of Heaven will be made up of individuals from every tribe, people and nation (Revelation 5:9).

It is a curious phenomenon that, when we break a bone, the place were the break occurred heals stronger than the surrounding bone that had never been broken. Why would Father design such a system? He could have made the healed break equally strong or even maybe less strong, but he designed it to be stronger. Might he be showing that unity is stronger than division? In Psalms, we read that Father is near the broken-hearted. There is something in the heart of Father to heal brokenness, which releases Kingdom power. A unified power that will supply the Kingdom forever. Unity is in Father's heart. Jesus prayed for Kingdom unity in John 17 when he asked that his followers would be unified as the Father and Jesus are unified (John 17:11). One reason the Kingdom will endure forever is because it will be based on divine unity and a restoration of creation that does not wear out and run down.

Jesus Reveals The Results Of The Kingdom

I suggest to you that the Kingdom will last forever; it will work on different physical principles than we see operating in the world today. From those principles we get a glimpse of Kingdom power in the Bible. While there is a future, completed aspect of the Kingdom, we should not forget that the Kingdom of God is present now. As Father's power and glory are revealed in us, then the Kingdom is expanded and established now and in preparation for Jesus' return and rule upon the earth.

Summary

We have hope in the world, not so much because of the world's potential, but we have hope because Jesus is giving to us glory that we will never lose. That glory, at times is revealed in works of power, referred to as miracles. We see people saved and transformed, others healed of physical difficulties, and still others delivered from demonic oppression. We must remember who we are, from whom we receive our provision, and that the power from Papa enables us to overcome inner evil (temptation), as well as deliver us from external evil. The great thing is that this Kingdom will endure forever, a concept that is simply foreign to our ability to comprehend.

Questions for Reflection

1. How might Kingdom power, glory, and eternity impact the way you approach your daily life?

2. In what ways do the truths expressed in the Lord's Prayer give you hope?

3. What steps can you take to move from attachment to the world that is passing away, to the Kingdom that will endure forever?

Jesus Reveals The Results Of The Kingdom

Papa, thank you for your revelation of the Kingdom through the Lord's Prayer. Give to us the wisdom to not only live according to the Lord's Prayer, but to discover and live out the yet-to-be revealed implications of this prayer. Amen.

Chapter 11
Conclusions

Jesus' teaching on prayer changed the whole understanding of prayer. Jesus' way of prayer was so unusual that the disciples sought him out and asked him to teach them to pray. Their request reveals that they recognized a deficiency in their own method. Remember that these were men who had been familiar with the prayers of the Old Testament and with John the Baptist's teaching on prayer. They knew how to pray according to the Old Testament, but still they sought more. Jesus taught them to approach God as Father. His teaching revealed how their Father in heaven loved them, so that they could come with great boldness and intimacy. This would have been unusual because, prior to that time, people would have approached God in fear or out of duty, with petitions, rather than declarations and commands.

It is ironic how often we Christians fall into an Old Testament model of prayer. Often we pray as if we have no intimacy with Father, as if He were still a distant God hidden behind a veil, so that we must petition, beg and convince Him to act on our behalf. This is not what Jesus taught about Father or the way to pray. His bold approach to prayer is so radically different than what many people expect, that some Christians cannot even admit that Jesus' prayers were grammatically commands and not requests. This hesitancy may result, although I hope not, in a continued estrangement that some Christians feel towards Father. They admit intellectually that Father loves them, but they do not live according to that truth and often do not pray according to that truth. Too many of us followers of Jesus fail to walk in the freedom that Jesus purchased for us on the cross (Galatians 5:1).

Jesus' initial instructions imply the responsibility that we have before Father on earth. It is our responsibility to pray/declare and command Father's name to be recognized as holy, His will to be exercised on earth in the same way it is in

Conclusions

heaven, and to expand His Kingdom upon the earth through prayer. By praying in this manner, Father makes us partners in the establishment and expansion of His Kingdom upon the earth. We are not passive in asking; Father supplies all the power, but our prayer is effectual in bringing our declarations to fruition. In our fast-paced world, where the only way to get anything done is through action, viewing prayer as a means of bringing something about seems very odd; yet this is the way the Kingdom of Heaven works. The Kingdom of Heaven does not work in the way the world works. It is not based on our efforts and gifts, but operates on our application of Kingdom truth.

The Lord's Prayer is also a reflection of Jesus' promise to meet the needs of his followers. We do not need to worry about what we will eat or wear, because as we focus our lives and energy upon the Kingdom of Heaven, Jesus promises to meet all of our physical, emotional and spiritual needs. He provides our daily bread, he provides forgiveness as we practice it, he protects us from evil and he empowers us to overcome the temptation to involve ourselves in evil. As we understand the Lord's Prayer, we discover that is is a model for living the Christian life and expanding the Kingdom.

There are concepts presented in this book that may seem radical. It is my hope that they have spurred your thinking so that you will seek an even deeper relationship with your Father in Heaven. He loves you and continually craves a more intimate relationship with you. I pray that they will sprout and lead you on to discover more Kingdom truths that have only been touched on in this book.

Endnotes

[1] Dana and Mantey, A Manual of Greek Grammar, pg 176

[2] Eusebius, Church History, v. 3, ch. 5